Stockhausen Serves Imperialism
and other articles

T0054449

CORNELIUS CARDEW

Stockhausen Serves Imperialism

and other articles

with commentary and notes

Primary Information

Contents

Introduction

This book raises more questions than it answers. Two questions in particular have repeatedly posed themselves :

1) What are the relations of production in the field of music in bourgeois society? This is a theoretical question and can be clarified by sifting through the mass of data and experience available. However, the urgency of this problem is debatable.

2) What is the relative importance and significance of polemics such as those documented in this book in the context of the class struggles surging around us in the imperialist heartlands today?

I will just comment briefly on these two questions in this introduction.

1) Because of the law of copyright (which is supposed to give authors and composers control over the exploitation of their works) on the one hand and the idealist image many an artist has of himself as a 'creator' on the other, there is a tendency to imagine that the composer or writer is a 'free producer', that his product belongs to him to do with as he sees fit. In fact, a book or a composition is not an end-product, not in itself a useful commodity. The end-product of an artist's work, the 'useful commodity' in the production of which he plays a role, is ideological influence. He is as incapable of producing this on his own as a blacksmith is of producing Concorde. The production of ideological influence is highly socialised, involving (in the case of music) performers, critics, impresarios, agents, managers, etc., and above all (and this is the artist's real 'means of production') an audience.

In bourgeois society, the artist is in the employ of capitalists (publishers, record companies), who demand from him work

7

that is, at least potentially, profitable. And ultimately he is in the employ of the bourgeois state, which demands that the artist's work be ideologically acceptable. Since the state controls our main organ of mass communication, the BBC, it can determine whether or not a work will be profitable by exercising its censorship. An example is Paul McCartney's 'Give Ireland Back to the Irish', which was all set to bring massive profits to the capitalists, had its exploitation not been drastically curtailed by a BBC ban. The capitalists took their cue and the song became hard to find.

If this is the fate of a sentimental pop song under the bourgeois dictatorship, it is clearly impossible to bring work with a decidedly socialist or revolutionary content to bear on a mass audience. Access to this audience (the artist's real means of production) is controlled by the state. This is why Marx and Engels say that the bourgeoisie have reduced artists to the level of wage-slaves (see page 100, note 6). The artist has a job, and the conditions of employment are laid down by the bourgeoisie.

2) In the age of large-scale industrial production, the largest, strongest and most revolutionary class is the industrial working class. Marxists hold (and this book has been put together from a Marxist standpoint) that the overthrow of the bourgeois dictatorship will be led (as it has been, historically, in various countries) by the working class. Hence it is the ideological trends current in the working class that merit attention rather than those current in the intelligentsia or other minority sections of the population. Obviously Cage, Stockhausen and the rest have no currency in the working class, so criticism of their work is relatively unimportant. In fact this whole polemical attack, including this book, takes place outside the working class movement and is therefore politically relatively insignificant.

However, though Cage and Stockhausen have no hold on the working class, they did have a strong hold on me, Tilbury and others whose views feature in this book, and doubtless they still have a strong hold on many of the potential readers of this book. The violence of the attack on them is indicative of the strength of their hold on us; a powerful wrench was required to liberate us from this particular entanglement.

Political consciousness does not come like a flash of lightning. It's a process that passes through a number of stages. The stage documented in this book may be deemed unnecessary as far as the working class is concerned, but it was necessary for us. The Scratch Orchestra (whose history I found myself unable to bring up to date without becoming speculative and hence decided to leave as it was) did in fact go on to new stages, for instance, a movement to criticise music and films that *do* have wide currency in the working class. People in the Scratch Orchestra also took the line of integrating with the workers and fighting alongside them, as opposed to standing on the sidelines and cheering them on, or taking a stand above them and lecturing them on what they should be doing. The struggle to put this line into practice is still going on.

For the musician, the process of integrating with the working class brings unavoidable involvement with the ideological trends current in that class, both at the receiving end, among the 'consumers' of pop music, etc., and at the production end, through leaving the avantgarde clique and integrating more with musicians working in the music 'industry' proper.

Integrating with the working class has two aspects : (a) integrating with the working class movement as a whole, and (b) integrating with the particular section of workers of which you are a member (in my case, working musicians). It is in the context of the second aspect that the clarification of the relations of production (point 1 above) has a certain importance. The first aspect brings another matter to the fore : the question of the political party of the proletariat, the vanguard Marxist-Leninist Party which stands for the interests of the working class as a whole, and without which the workers will not be able to topple the dictatorship of the bourgeoisie, seize political power and establish the Dictatorship of the Proletariat. (Today, because of the efforts of the new Tsars of the Soviet Union – phoney 'communists' like Khrushchev and Brezhnev – to subvert the whole terminology of Communism and 'revise' Marxism for bourgeois ends, it is necessary to specify the political line of a Communist Party and draw a sharp distinction between Marxist-Leninist and revisionist parties.)

The 'study of Marxism and of society', which Mao Tsetung places alongside the question of integrating with the masses as an essential part of the work of class-conscious artists and intellectuals, leads swiftly to the realisation of the necessity of

9

building this proletarian Party. It also makes it clear that a genuine proletarian and revolutionary art will only develop under the leadership of such a Party. Without such a Party, every effort on the part of progressive artists to produce revolutionary art is bound to be relatively isolated and relatively ineffective. This is not to say it is wrong to make these efforts, any more than it is wrong to go on strike because the gains therefrom will be limited and not 'revolutionary'. To discourage such efforts is to negate struggle and weaken the impetus of workers (whether intellectual or industrial) to change society. It is precisely through such struggles that political consciousness is aroused. Both ideological and economic struggles prepare the ground for building the revolutionary Party of the Proletariat.

As for this book: as a thing in itself, it can be seen as irrelevant to the working class movement. But no book is a 'thing-in-itself'; if this book gives background and perspectives to a particular form of class struggle in a particular situation, and shows this as something which is not static and final but developing from a particular point of departure through various phases to a new stage with wider perspectives; if this book can be read and understood in this way then its purpose will have been achieved.

I have provided continuity material (in italics) linking the various documents, and a number of notes (at the end of the book) to clarify references in the text. These notes are not subordinate to the texts, in fact they are often corrective to the texts and represent a later, firmer standpoint. Consequently, I would like them to be read with equal attention and as an integral part of the book.

As regards the arrangement of the chapters, the Scratch Orchestra History is like a spring-board from which the critical articles jump off. The Criticism of Cage and Stockhausen began about the time the History ends (May 1972). The subsequent history of the Scratch Orchestra has provided even more food for thought than the early history and I would like to have given an account of it (it would also have provided more context for the last two chapters), but, as I've said, this has proved impossible.

C.C., 14.6.74

CHAPTER 1

A History of the Scratch Orchestra
1969–72

At a certain stage in the development of the Scratch Orchestra the politically more conscious members (constituted within the Orchestra as the Ideological Study Group) felt the need to clarify our experience in the Orchestra, to view it historically and sum it up. We therefore commissioned Rod Eley, the most educated among us, to write the History of the Scratch Orchestra. He based his work on written reports submitted by a number of individuals who had first-hand experience of the various stages of the Orchestra's work. I have added notes at the end of the book to clarify references that would otherwise be meaningless.

A HISTORY OF THE SCRATCH ORCHESTRA
by ROD ELEY

The origins of the Scratch Orchestra derive from the Experimental Music Class at Morley College (1) run by Cornelius Cardew and attended by a number of young composers, some of whom were also pupils of Cardew at the Royal Academy of Music. In May 1969 Victor Schonfield put on a 7-hour concert, including among other things Cardew's *Great Learning Paragraph 2* and John Cage's *Atlas Eclipticalis. Paragraph 2* brought together over 50 people around the nucleus of the Morley College class. Seizing the moment, and seeing the potential of this large group and the need of the members of the group for outlets for their ideas and activity, Cardew wrote the *Draft Constitution*, founded the Scratch Orchestra together with Michael Parsons and Howard Skempton, and opened its bank account. The *Draft Constitution* (2) was published in the

Musical Times in June 1969 and a meeting of interested people was called for July 1st. Practical work began in September and the first public concerts in November.

In this initial phase of formation one can detect some of the seeds of future growth, deeply embedded contradictions within the Orchestra which have been sharpening ever since. The nucleus of Morley College composers were dissatisfied with 'established, serious' music; in other words, they were dissatisfied with the elitism of 'serious' music and its strong class image, and with the repression of working musicians into the role of slavish hacks churning out the stock repertoire of concert hall and opera house. The prevailing dry, limited critical approach in this century had for them killed spontaneity and simple enjoyment of music and reduced it to an academic and self-conscious 'appreciation' of form and technique. In the *Draft Constitution* the category of Popular Classics – where famous but now hackneyed classics were given unorthodox and irreverent interpretations – was a blow against the crippling orthodoxy of 'musical taste'. The attraction of a number of non-reading musicians and actual non-musicians into the Orchestra through seeing the *Draft Constitution* was therefore welcomed. Here was a source of ideas and spontaneity less hampered by academic training and inhibitions. Amongst the Scratch Orchestra members there was considerable support for the ideas of John Cage, Christian Wolff, etc.; that is, random music with a multiplicity of fragments without cohesion, as opposed to serialism. Aleatory (chance) music seemed richer, unpredictable, free! But serialism, the tradition stemming from Schönberg, was formal, abstract and authoritarian. Most important was the social implication of Cage's work – the idea that we are all musical, that 'anybody can play it'. All this, at least, in theory. Serial music, on the other hand, was definitely elitist, uncompromisingly bourgeois, and anti-people. From the first, music was considered an experience which might include other media.

However, while rejecting the formal preoccupations of 'serial' music, the Scratch Orchestra was still formalist. Whilst eager to tap new sources of vitality, to experiment with compositions that had the character of catalysts, stimulating the sensitivity, imagination and inventiveness of the members, the content of the music was invariably reactionary. The concern was to create 'beautiful experiences'. The problem was really one of form.

What bound together the varied membership of the Scratch Orchestra? A common experience of the two oppressive blocs in our social and cultural environment – the 'serious' music and art of the establishment on the one hand, and the commercialism of pop, etc., on the other. However, the struggle against them was blind and instinctual rather than conscious at this stage. A number of Orchestra members did think in terms of the Orchestra as a subversion of bourgeois cultural and social values, as have a couple of generations of young artists. But their cultural 'protest' took much the same form as before: music was to be experienced for its own sake. It was the stock reaction of the alienated, bourgeois artist – withdrawal from social responsibility – 'art for art's sake'. At its worst the roots of the ambitions of the Orchestra lay in the Romantic pretension, expressed by Keats: 'All art aspires to the condition of music'. Music being a 'pure experience', untainted by mundane human or social concerns.

Thus the inception of the Scratch Orchestra was an unconscious and, as it eventually came to appear, a negative, self-indulgent and basically reactionary rejection of the culture and values of the ruling class, of bourgeoisie. No one as yet understood that *both* these oppressive blocs – bourgeois establishment culture and pop commercialism – were only two facets of *one* world-wide system of oppression: the capitalist system, and its final stage, imperialism, now degenerating into fascism throughout the so-called 'free world'. We were all unconsciously rejecting imperialist art, art as a commodity for sale on the market, a function which has been developed since Renaissance times with the rise to power of the bourgeoisie, but which has now reached the point of bankruptcy. It is now an art whose sole function is to shore up the decaying superstructure in an attempt to stave off the inevitable collapse of imperialism. With the gradual breakdown of the capitalist world during the twentieth century the future life of the bourgeoisie, the preservation of their illgotten wealth, has become one incredible mass of problems for them. This is seen in personal anxiety and neuroses due to alienation, the pressure of the 'rat-race' and now a growing sense of guilt or, to be more accurate, fear about the precarious affluence of a small class in a sea of world poverty; a world of growing unrest, communist subversion and revolution, national

13

wars and the threat of a Third World War, from which they know they could not survive. As all political efforts fail to check this collapse, the bourgeois ideologists – so-called economists, social 'scientists' and other 'experts' – are busily constructing Malthusian theories of doom, reducing man to a lemming-like creature set on its own destruction. In this way they try to make universal the approaching doom of capitalism and the bourgeoisie, and transform it by an academic conjuring trick into the doom of the entire world, or at least 'civilisation', as they would have it. Bourgeois artists have thus abstracted their own predicament from its class context and turned it into the 'human predicament'. This is why the key-note of 'serious' art this century in the capitalist world has been profound pessimism – the product : negative nihilistic art. Less honest bourgeois art has been more or less on the level of trivial fantasy. Bourgeois art of all kinds has been ignored by the working class for the most part. To them it has not even had the titillating appeal of scandal which it has had, at times, for the bourgeoisie and petty bourgeoisie. But even that effect has diminished; today 'anything goes', and usually unheard and unseen! Recent music is disliked, significantly, by working musicians.

The achievement of the great bourgeois composers such as Beethoven was to make the composer 'independent' from feudal patronage (3). Now he sold his product in the market like any producer. But he had to compete for custom with other artists. His music had to be marked with a strong individual musical style in order to sell – a kind of brand name. With the trend towards individualism also came the removal of the composer from direct social contact with his audience. In the open market, or to be more exact, in the world of music publishers, agents, concert and theatre impresarios, you either had the saleable product or nothing. Relations were strictly on a cash basis. So the composer became alienated from his product or music, and from the audience. This explains the trend of 'serious art' towards abstraction. The audience capable of following such music has diminished. Most composers in that tradition can now only make a living by teaching or pumping out music for TV commercials or background music for films. Such 'serious' composition as is done has been reduced to an almost entirely private, 'Sunday' activity amongst a few receptive friends and for minute public audiences (mostly consisting of the very same friends) (4).

This brings us to a most important point. The Scratch Orchestra was formed because a number of friends – people with similar artistic interests and attitudes – and who happened to find a focal point in the figure of Cardew, had grown to the point where the formation of a large-scale group was a natural (but not mechanically predestined) response to the demands of social necessity. In addition it was recognised from the outset that there are growing numbers of people (mostly young) with the same reaction to cultural oppression as us. That is why the *Draft Constitution* said 'the Scratch Orchestra intends to function in the public sphere'.

How can we explain this large, and apparently increasing, pool of dissatisfied young people?

'The lower strata of the middle class . . . sink gradually into the proletariat, partly because their diminutive capital does not suffice for the scale on which modern industry is carried on, and is swamped in competition with the large capitalists, partly because their specialised skill is rendered worthless by new methods of production.' . . . 'Further, as we have seen already, entire sections of the ruling classes are, by the advance of industry, precipitated into the proletariat, or are at least threatened in their conditions of existence.' (Karl Marx and Friederich Engels, *Communist Manifesto*, 1848.)

What new methods of production have rendered our specialised skill, as creative musicians, worthless? Quite obviously, the application of technology to music: records, the tape recorder, radio, television, and the electronic amplification of instruments. As a matter of fact the number of properly employed professional musicians in this country, and in general throughout the capitalist world, has actually diminished (5), despite larger population and a claimed raising of cultural standards with more widespread education.

Why? Because live musicians are a more expensive means of producing music than machines. The object of the entrepreneur in music, as in the production and sale of all commodities, is to reduce labour costs. For in capitalism the profit is derived from the surplus value of human labour; that is the value of the amount produced over and above that necessary to provide a living wage to the worker. This is clearly seen throughout the capitalist world in the application of technology and sociological efficiency techniques, like work study. The result is greater productivity, certainly. A man can produce with a machine what it may have taken 100 men before. But for whose benefit is the advance made? In the case of music, the claim that the reduction of manpower by new technology is to reduce 'drudgery' is seen for what it really is in all fields – hypocritical rubbish! Today the opportunity for people with musical talent, or other artistic ability, to play a productive part in society is shrinking to vanishing point. The vast mass of music heard is produced by machines and their machine-minders – the disc jockeys. Even in the field of 'serious' music orchestral players are ground down to a monotonous repertoire of eighteenth and nineteenth century classics, and often feel little better than hacks. For those in the 'live' field of popular music, for the older generation there is constant mechanical repetition of 'old favourites'; for the young there is the domination of the entire capitalist world by a few British and American groups; everyone has to dance to their tune.

In addition, the continued expansion of monopoly capital is every day threatening the small capitalists and the 'professional' classes, i.e. the petty bourgeoisie (6). Dissatisfaction has spread widely throughout the petty bourgeois youth and students in Britain, Ireland, America and Europe, witness the spontaneous upsurge of the student movement against American imperialism in Vietnam in the 1960s. Hitherto, when the capitalist system was strong the petty bourgeoisie trailed behind the bourgeoisie. Now that the world's oppressed people are rising up to wipe out imperialism, this class is vacillating and many youth and students are disillusioned and unwilling to take up their role as servants of monopoly capital. They are searching around for a better role (7).

This then is the source of the rapidly increasing pool of dissatisfied young people from which the Scratch Orchestra is drawn and to which it has tended to appeal: the decay of the British bourgeoisie under the impact of growing working class militancy, seen in factory occupations, massive wage demands and strikes; as part of the general pattern of crisis in the world capitalist system through the accumulation of internal contradictions and national liberation movements in the so-called Third World. Bourgeois ideology and education attempt to make some sense of the world, a world 'safe for capitalism'. The contrast with the objective facts is glaring. The bourgeois world outlook is in ruins, along with capitalism.

From the first, the Scratch Orchestra has therefore been a truly 'social' body, a product of social and historical change, not a formal body which would collapse with the desertion of some members. The majority of the members were petty bourgeois students and intellectuals with a genuine, serious and principled interest in finding out what was the right way to contribute to society. Active membership in the region of forty to sixty has been maintained by constant infusion of new blood.

The first active phase of public performances was from November 1969 to July 1970. There were seven concerts from November to January, six during April–May, and one in June plus a BBC studio recording of paragraph 2 of Cardew's *Great Learning*. The culmination of this period was the two-week tour – 27 July to 7 August 1970 – playing to country audiences in village halls, etc., the first week in Cornwall, the second in Anglesey, North Wales. Some members now look back on that whole period as the 'Golden Age' of the Scratch Orchestra.

It was certainly a period of great energy and optimism. The *Draft Constitution* proved its strength; concerts *were* put on. In addition new elements accrued which extended the scope of the Orchestra, and pointed the way to the future development of social involvement. These elements were:

1) Spontaneously and collectively designed programmes to cater for colleges which invited us to play (in contrast to the central idea of the *Draft Constitution*, which was concerts proposed by individual members).

2) Participation in two political events: the Chicago 8 Protest Concert (8) and a Campaign for Nuclear Disarmament Rally.

3) The beginning of a movement towards 'environmental events': a well-planned all-day ambulatory concert round the Richmond area, designed by Psi Ellison and Stefan Szczelkun, and a concert in the forecourt of Euston railway station.

Two important lessons emerged from this 'Golden Age', however. At the Chicago 8 concert, which was mainly a pop event, it was clear that a band of 100 players without discipline was actually weaker than a disciplined band of ten or even five. The other discovery was that, despite some TV coverage in December 1969 in addition to the many concerts, the Scratch Orchestra did not catch on with the public. And in fact to this day almost the only occasions when the Orchestra can count on a large audience are at intermittent performances of Cardew's *Great Learning* (roughly three times a year), and much rarer performances of works by Christian Wolff, etc.; and this is due almost entirely to the reputation of the composer, not the Scratch Orchestra, and the publicity grapevine of Victor Schonfield's Music Now organisation, which spreads its tendrils amongst the 'progressive', avantgarde elements of the musical 'establishment'. Although if you take the country as a whole there are large numbers who have heard of the Scratch Orchestra – amongst art students and the like interested in the avantgarde – only on exceptional occasions such as the Liverpool concert (January 1972) has the audience been large on the strength of the Orchestra's reputation. Perhaps because of the odd locations of many of our events and the frequent disappointment of those who do see us we have mostly outnumbered the audience. There seem to be, as yet, few regular Scratch concert-goers.

Why then did the Scratch Orchestra not disintegrate through lack of the encouragement of public support, lack of direction and its own internal ultra-democracy?

1) Ironically, the usual need for public support (and thus the search for audience) – the need for money – was no problem. The fees from TV and a number of concerts at arts festivals and the like, supported by the Arts Council and similar funds, that is by the state and private industry, have proved sufficient to meet the expenses of travel, publicity and the staging of other ventures as well. No member of the Orchestra received fees for performances. All our appearances were financial failures, judged on a profit-loss basis, but could be subsidised from the earnings of a few avantgarde concerts, smiled on by the establishment. Thus the bourgeois ruling class, which in every other case, even where human life is at stake, demands that everything should 'pay its way' or 'realise a profit', in the case of avantgarde culture is prepared to corrupt any potential threat to the worship of dead idols and present-day mediocrity, tame it, and thus house-trained, actively promote such rubbish – bourgeois liberal, idealistic,

anarchistic and nihilistic art. Thus with the Scratch Orchestra. While the merry-go-round continued to turn there was no concern with winning an audience, or, as it was usually put, 'making concessions to the public'. Thus also there was no idea that the Orchestra must grow, gain strength and improve . . . develop or die. The activity was an end in itself. In this way the capitalist system, now in its terminal stage, deludes people with an imaginary world without change, either growth or decay, where money – the 'cash nexus' which alone links humans together in social relationships amongst the bourgeoisie; money – the 'god' of capitalist society – is thought to have the mystical property of sustaining life itself in near corpses. State or industrial subsidy is to the arts in the bourgeois world what expensive medical technology, like heart transplants, is to the moribund. The function of bourgeois art at this stage is not to make bourgeois society seem any brighter (that is now impossible) but to make it universal – so that pessimism, defeatism and nihilism are seen to be rooted in 'Man'.

2) However, although this financial support did ensure survival in the early stages, this aspect was not absolutely fundamental. The Scratch Orchestra was not constituted with a clearly defined aim, like most cultural groups, whether to play the blues or avantgarde music. It fulfilled a deeper social need for a number of people who were already involved in that kind of activity in many cases. In a kind of blind way it was known from the first, and can be seen in the scope of the *Draft Constitution* with its spur to research projects that the Scratch Orchestra had some functional role in present-day social change. As yet this was only glimpsed in bourgeois idealism, the search for some ideal way of organising people to a common task without infringing their 'individuality' or establishing any hierarchy to the detriment of 'equality': some vague anarchism lay at the root, with its starry-eyed faith in 'human nature if freed from authority', the abstraction of human nature from its class context.

3) The *Draft Constitution* was the unifying factor. It provided a stimulating base from which to organise concerts. It encouraged ideas, composition and activities which drew together all the disparate elements of the membership.

4) The quality of leadership by Cardew was another important factor which held the Orchestra together. It vindicates the

19

Marxist concept of natural leadership; the idea that human groups provide the leaders appropriate to the realisation of their needs. Certainly this does not mean the 'Führer principle' – the bogey which so many 'democratic' liberals see in the term 'leadership'. No, this leadership has been neither imposed, nor induced by some personality cult, but by the way in which Cardew and the *Draft Constitution* he wrote managed, for a time, to channel the aspirations and activities of a body of people in a way meaningful to all of them, which brought out the best in them. Cardew's role in the orchestra has been important, but it must not be exaggerated. Indeed, the manner of leadership in the Orchestra is now in the process of change as we search out a new role in society. In the end, leadership is only the guiding element in a more fundamental social trend. The true potential strength of the Scratch Orchestra lies with the membership, and its future reflection of the militant, revolutionary aspirations and struggle of the proletariat in an artistic form.

The *Draft Constitution* was the last word in liberalism. 'Anything goes' was the policy and any discussion of the merits of a proposal was outlawed. However, this had a beneficial aspect, for the Constitution stressed the importance of actually organising activities. This was a break with sterile and detached preoccupations with 'criticism' which paralyse and degenerate most bourgeois art movements. In this atmosphere a kind of *collective confidence* grew out of the common activity of work together. Instead of one or two individuals doing everything, new and younger people were encouraged to put their ideas into practice, and this released a lot of initiative. By encouraging the active participation of everyone, individualism was opposed and this created fertile conditions for the introduction of the new ideas of Marxism-Leninism. The respect for real work, actual leadership and for putting ideas into practice made many members receptive to the Marxist-Leninist principle of integrating theory with practice in order to change society, and working as a collective.

All these factors, then, enabled the Scratch Orchestra to establish, during the initial 'Golden Age' (November 1969 to July 1970) the resilience of a complex network of personal relationships, generating a sense of equality and mutual respect amongst the membership through the experience of much work done in common at many concerts, that has enabled it to survive so many disappointments and the threat of collapse through internal contradictions. During this initial phase of hectic growth which firmly established a sense of 'Scratch identity' the Orchestra was not yet forced to face those contradictions; therefore it developed in a positive and fruitful way for the time being.

In fact there were already factors at work which would bring this honeymoon atmosphere to an end; or perhaps we should say, which marked a new development since, strictly speaking, there have been no 'beginnings', no 'ends', no clearly defined periods but a continuous process of change from which we are trying to extract formative trends and find the points where the development took significant steps forward.

The village hall concert tour at the turn of July–August 1970 seemed to sum up the achievement of Scratch Orchestra identity. Here was a group of Scratchers, relaxed and with a wealth of shared experience, working and alert to learn more. Amongst the Orchestra there was diminishing interest in the formal concert. In the country the Scratch came across a different kind of audience. The reception was friendly and good-natured by people who had not heard of Cage or Stockhausen. People joined in and played with the Scratchers. People in the country seemed to have the self-assurance and emotional maturity to enable them to accommodate this 'foreign body'. This was in stark contrast to the crippling inhibition and alienation amongst the usual audiences in London and in colleges – the 'respectable' and the 'intellectual', the bourgeois and the petty bourgeois (9).

At the time the reaction of the Orchestra was to lay blame for this failure on the audience, the common vice of the 'avantgarde' bourgeois through this century. What was not realised was that in the village hall tour we had encountered a *different class*, the rural proletariat. But an accumulation of similar experiences, for instance with bystanders at later environmental events in towns who were usually working class adults and children, gradually made some members aware of the class basis of culture, through our education at the hands of audiences : on the one hand there was the inhibited, passively 'appreciative', intellectual reaction of the bourgeois and petty bourgeois; on the other hand the more relaxed, spontaneous and honest reaction of the proletariat. Eventually some members came to fully understand through practical experience (not theory alone) this correct analysis of culture by Mao Tsetung :

'In the world today all culture, all literature and art belong to definite classes and are geared to definite political lines. There is in fact no such thing as art for art's sake, art that stands above classes, art that is detached from or independent of politics.' (*Talks at the Yenan Forum on Literature and Art,* 1942.)

With September 1970 we enter the second phase of the Scratch Orchestra's development. It began in a spirit of great optimism after the village hall tour, and ended in the disillusionment and recriminations of the Discontent Meetings of August 1971. During this period the hitherto submerged contradictions already outlined began to sharpen and break through the hardening crust of the 'old' Scratch Orchestra. There were six concerts in November, six in December 1970, mostly in universities, art colleges and concert halls. But a change was on the way, with more environmental work, and work impinging on society and the community after Christmas. A section of the Orchestra were increasingly attracted by the challenge of this kind of activity, and they began to make the pace in the production of concert proposals. But disillusionment was to come, with the fiasco at the Metro Club, Notting Hill, in 12 June 1971. Here we were faced with a club for young immigrants, oppressed by the bourgeois ruling class and therefore the natural enemy of capitalist society. There had been several arrests in a riot with the police at the club the previous week and there was a display board of telegrams and messages of support from black liberation movements the world over. What did the Scatch Orchestra produce? A *Toy Symphony* – a typical Scratch atavism, return to childhood. We experienced at last the true nature of our almost total incompetence, and the total irrelevance of the Scratch Orchestra in its present form in the modern world (10). But even with this experience, social awareness, and therefore the awareness of the futility of everything we stood for – bourgeois art and society – did not come yet (except for the Communist members who were to provide leadership into the next stage). It did not come until we ourselves, as an orchestra, were the direct victims of this same social and cultural oppression experienced daily by black people and the working class throughout the 'free world'. This blow, which finally brought the Scratch Orchestra to its senses, was to fall within a fortnight of the Metro Club fiasco, when it went on tour to Newcastle, Durham and the North East from 21–26 June 1971. But we will come to that later.

Two features of this period must be noted. The first was the gathering rival attraction of the so-called Scratch subgroups (generally agreed to be a misnomer). As the problems of Scratch Orchestra development became greater many of the 'musicians' tended to devote increasing attention to their small groups, such as PTO, Harmony Band and Private Company, to name a sample (11). Such parallel development had for a time its good points; it was natural to try out ideas with the confidence gained through Scratch Orchestra experience, in more manageable groups of fewer numbers and greater homogeneity. However, as a result, a definite decline in new ideas and composition for the Scratch Orchestra did take place, and this in turn dispirited people who wanted to get on performing new compositions, and who favoured music in the concert hall to social involvement with the environment.

The second, and complementary feature of this reduction in 'musical' content was the rise of the 'non-musicians' to take the initiative largely vacated by the 'musicians'. The appearances of the Scratch Orcestra had always had the character of 'Happenings', but now this more provocative role (playing aboard trains in the Underground, etc.) became predominant; and it was accompanied by diminishing attendance by many orchestra members at public appearances, especially amongst the 'musicians'. However, as always, performances of Cardew's *Great Learning*, for instance Paragraphs 2 and 7 for a recording by Deutsche Grammophon on 15 February 1971, for their series Avant Garde; and other Paragraphs at St Pancras Church on 17 April 1971, for the Camden Arts Festival; and at the Wandel Concert at the German Institute on 13 May 1971; these events brought Scratchers back together to work sometimes for a number of weeks of rehearsal before performance. So the rupture between 'musicians' and 'non-musicians' was contained. In fact the polarisation of the groups did not go too far, and there were always people playing a positive role in Scratch development with a foot in both camps. As with the case of 'periods' of development, 'musicians' and 'non-musicians' were not discrete

23

entities; we use them rather to distinguish divergent tendencies within the Orchestra.

Now it is necessary to describe the events of this period in more detail to bring the experience of the Orchestra (and thus our analysis) to life.

After the village concerts of July–August 1970 the Scratch Orchestra went back to routine concerts, and the audience reaction compared unfavourably. Except for the first appearance at the German Institute on 11 December 1970, organised by Greg Bright, which was well-rehearsed and where we were playing to an audience tuned in to avantgarde music, audience alienation was often painfully obvious; for instance at the Queen Elizabeth Hall concert of 23 November 1970 (12), and at Leeds and Essex Universities on 27 and 28 November. It was probably as a natural reaction to disappointing contact with the audience that a group emerged within the Orchestra – the self-dubbed Slippery Merchants – which organised, in secret, events to occur coincidentally during Scratch concerts. On 'aesthetic' grounds this could be seen as an extension of the tradition of John Cage – randomness and simultaneity. The intervention of the Merchants thus added an unexpected note of drama at some concerts and as a result provided newsworthy items for reporters or critics, desperate to find something they could understand – sensation – for their papers, on the occasions they were present, as at the Queen Elizabeth Hall concert. Perhaps it did not strike too many of the 'musicians' at the time, but for the audience the appearance of the Slippery Merchants in strange attire and performing inexplicable actions more or less completely swamped interest in the music.

Were the Slippery Merchants a valuable development for the Scratch Orchestra? In the end, yes. Because although their activities were finally to prove negative and vacuous (they were to disband themselves by April 1971) they did serve to sharpen the contradictions within the Scratch Orchestra, and therefore probably accelerated the ensuing crisis of the 'old' Scratch Orchestra.

The Slipperies often moved in among the audience at concerts, initially in the manner of clowns at the circus to bring contact with the audience down to a personal face-to-face level, incidentally providing good fun; but increasingly to talk to people, and this was a positive step. At Scratch meetings they proposed many

24

events to happen in public places, on the grounds that random and surprising appearances of people playing music and dressed in some amazing costume, or Wig Out as they called it, would shock people, if only for a short while, out of their alienation into a deeper awareness of each other. The School Raids (sudden, clandestine swoops on school playgrounds round London) were an example of this. And in future Scratch activities, even though formally disbanded as a group, the Slipperies' ideas came strongly to the fore, partly because of the dearth of alternatives. There was the Primrose Hill Walk organised by Catherine Williams on 15 May 1971, and the three events of Birgit Burckhardt: Scratch Below, which consisted of random appearances on the tube or subway, taking place over the whole day of 19 May 1971; the Demolition Site Event to attract the children of a working class locality on May 22nd; and the event where the Scratch Orchestra attempted to 'merge with Highgate Cemetery' on May 29th – paying our respects at the grave of Karl Marx, almost in unconscious anticipation of the future turn of events in the Orchestra. These experiences, notably the Tube Event, were important in stimulating social awareness, and consequently the questioning of the role of an orchestra such as ours in society today.

It is curious how vividly such environmental events – with their unexpected encounters and crazy situations – remain in the memory, although they were failures in reality, compared to the more formal, characteristic 'Scratch Music' presentations in concert halls; that is for those who were there, and by now many of the original people were absent from these latest developments, the point of growth and conflict. This split in experience, which had been shared previously, goes far to explain the problem of healing the rift within the Orchestra which is still current. Those of us who are reluctant to abandon 'old' Scratch idealism and anarchy tend to be the people with least experience of this kind of event.

But the vacuity of the trend of these events began to weigh heavily on everyone. Take for instance the environmental event composed by Hugh Shrapnel, which took place on and below some dramatic cliffs on the Dorset coast in February 1971. What did it achieve? It was in many ways a beautiful experience, but largely because of the sheer amazing good fortune of the weather;

the day turned out like a clear, warm day in mid-summer, ideal for cooking in the open, scrambling round rocks, etc. But who could share the experience? The seagulls, who echoed with their cries the Bach Prelude of a solitary cellist playing on a remote crag! And one or two incurious cliff walkers. Although some of the more formal avantgarde concerts seemed to bring periodic revival of the old spirit, for instance Greg Bright's *Balkan Sobranie Smoking Mixture* concert at Ealing Town Hall on 25 February 1971, and the Wandel Concert at the German Institute on 13 May, people became generally discouraged even with the 'old' Scratch music.

Things came to a head quite quickly when the crisis came. On June 12th there was the unnerving experience at the Metro Club. Then came the tour of the North East – of notorious memory – from June 21–26th five concerts arranged and sponsored by Northern Arts. At the very first, at the Newcastle Civic Centre, the civic authorities intervened and forced the abandonment of the concert on the grounds of obscenity. Cardew, in accordance with the instructions of Greg Bright's piece *Sweet F.A.*, was writing four-letter words (now apparently permissible on TV) on toilet paper. In addition they banned us from returning to the Newcastle Civic Centre, as had already been arranged, for the final concert of the tour. The local and then the national press scented scandal (and something to fill up their papers, because it was the 'silly season' when there is little political news). For the rest of the tour the Scratch Orchestra was hounded by the press, and the Sunderland concert was disrupted by newsmen. In a concentrated and vivid way the corruption, hypocrisy and worthlessness of the 'establishment' – the decaying, senile bourgeois ruling class – was rammed home in personal experience. The drivelling reports in the papers were a mixture of downright lies and ludicrous distortions in an effort to infuse sensation into our harmless activities. For instance: 'A man dressed in an ankle-length leather coat and wearing a beret was playing with plastic cups and writing obscene words on toilet paper. I saw a group of young children playing around his feet. It turned out to be Cornelius Cardew, a modern composer and leader of the Scratch Orchestra.' This was laughable, but this smear campaign to discredit Cardew as a composer had its sinister side, with the attempt to drag the Royal Academy of Music into the

26

scandal, hoping to strip him of his status as Professor of Composition.

The hypocrisy of local councillors, civic dignitaries and other lackeys of the ruling class became very clear as they spoke pompously of 'defending the civic dignity of Newcastle', with the inevitable reiteration of the cost of the Civic Centre (five million pounds), and the waste of 'public funds', 'tax-payers' money' on Scratch Orchestra expenses (£150 but reported as £250). All this to stir hatred of the Scratch Orchestra in particular, and of 'avantgarde, rebel intellectuals and lofties' in general. What on earth was our crime? All this in an area which has consistently shown some of the highest unemployment figures in the country every year since the Depression years of the '30s! And this itself is due, as is the decline of bourgeois culture, to the decline of the British bourgeoisie and the decay of British monopoly capitalism.

But of course the oppression we experienced was trivial. Our worst experience was to be thrown off the land where we were camping by the landlord who came to read of our activities. Although trivial compared to the material insecurity and deprivation and the psychological degradation forced by capitalism on millions of working class people, especially in the so-called 'underdeveloped' countries, this experience was enough, as Marx put it, to make us feel 'at least threatened in (our) conditions of existence'. Most important, it was an experience of oppression, not as individuals which many young feel today, but as an orchestra for the first time. In the excitement (and humour) of the situation the barriers to discussion began to fall (.13). The role of the Orchestra, its position in relation to the class struggle, was now in the process of being defined – in the usual way class is defined, by the oppressor. A group of genial eccentrics (you might call us) were under attack from established authority. Why? Previously without political awareness as a group, the politicisation of the Scratch Orchestra was begun. From this moment the 'old' Scratch Orchestra was dead; it merely remained to bury it. Perhaps significantly, but certainly unconsciously, Michael Chant's proposal had been adopted for the format of the Newcastle tour: the Dealer Concert concept. By this all existing, unused Scratch proposals were used up in one great welter of simultaneity.

27

Recognition of the crisis was confirmed with the project to build a cottage as an environment for activity, designed by Stefan Szczelkun, for the contribution of the Scratch Orchestra to the Arts Spectrum Exhibition at Alexandra Palace for two weeks in August. As Michael Chant says of this :

'The Orchestra could pull together sufficiently to build a fire-hazard, unfit for human habitation, and then withdraw to write its discontents. It became apparent that, like the cottage, the Orchestra was just a shell without any real substance.'

The contradictions, which had sharpened over two years, burst out with the Discontent Meetings of 23 and 24 August 1971. John Tilbury led in positively by presenting a Marxist analysis of the deterioration and vacuity of bourgeois cultural activity, as part of the general picture of social and political decay within the capitalist world today, but with particular reference to the Scratch Orchestra. Under this stimulus the Scratch Orchestra began to polarise into two groups : the 'Communists' and the 'bourgeois idealists', the latter composing a wide range of more or less nebulous and contradictory views.

What, precisely, was the line put forward by John Tilbury?

'After two years of activity, during which the whole gamut of contemporary bourgeois art has been explored, the Scratch Orchestra has reached an impasse. Either you sell your product on the market, or you drop out; this constitutes the dilemma of the bourgeois artist. The function of the Scratch Orchestra, if it is to remain bourgeois, is the mystification and further intensification of this dilemma, which is abstracted from its class context, universalised, and thus becomes "Man's Dilemma".'

Tilbury asked Mao Tsetung's question : Whom do we serve, which class do we support? Answer : clearly, the ruling class of the bourgeoisie. What was the reaction of those who feared the Communist line? As Tilbury says :

'Bourgeois idealism in the Scratch Orchestra, represented by anarchists and liberals, is characterised by simple accumulation of activities, fragmentation, and separation of ideas; and above all, by a pathological disunity between theory and practice." That is to say : despite the pious intentions of members to make contact with people, they were unable to carry them out in practice. Many different approaches were tried, but in a haphazard manner. Since there was no scientific base, no theory, no means of judging practice, they remained at the level of gimmicks, and certainly did not represent proper research into the problem of audience. Our files were full of proposed events that no one looked at again for the most part.

How could the Orchestra go forward? It should develop '. . . a revolutionary, Communist line using the method of Marxism and postulating dialectical change, the fusion and struggle of ideas and, most crucially, that (in the words of Mao Tsetung) "our thinking and feelings be changed and remoulded by gradually shedding our bourgeois world outlook and acquiring the proletarian, Communist outlook".' (14)

The clarity of the communist line put forward by John Tilbury and Keith Rowe brought together a smallish, but ideologically powerful group, containing Cornelius Cardew and some others of the most loyal and energetic Scratchers. They set up an Ideology Group to meet on a fortnightly basis; it set out, as Tilbury says, 'to study the works of the great revolutionary leaders, primarily Marx, Lenin and Mao Tsetung, in order to attack and expose the cultural superstructure of imperialism, with particular reference to music in England, and to evolve music and music-making which would serve the working and oppressed people of England.'

The approach of the group to its own development and its role in the Orchestra could be summed up in the slogan: 'Unity – Criticism – Unity'. That is to say, a deliberate, long-term view of the future of the Scratch Orchestra was taken. There could be no miraculous transformation. Only steady work and progress step by step could carry the Scratch Orchestra forward.

The stimulus of the Ideology Group has proved a challenge to many of the active members who remain unconvinced, even suspicious and afraid of the demand by the 'Communists' that the Scratch Orchestra get involved actively in the class struggle. Fruitful and healthy competition developed between the 'Communists' and 'bourgeois idealists'. From 30 August to 3 September 1971 a Summer School was held to raise the level of musical knowledge, instrumental technique and composition. John Tilbury gave a talk on Marxism, the first open effort to raise the political consciousness of the Orchestra. And even though it had been planned before the Discontents, and with a view to the education of the public (who never materialised), this Summer School represented (if in an embryonic form) a new development amongst the old Morley College nucleus, away from randomness and 'freedom' towards music organised to express some intended content. From September this trend became conscious, with regular meetings of the Scratch Orchestra (with quite a number of enthusiastic newcomers) on a weekly basis to practise music, and thus encourage the flow of new pieces and raise the level of public performance by proper rehearsal for concerts. The next Scratch appearance was not scheduled till January so that the Orchestra had time to rehearse, and consolidate the lessons learnt from the summer crisis. To this end, every third week's meeting was to be devoted to discussion of the compositions, the problem of the audience (what sort, how to reach it, how we could serve it), and thus further the process of political education and establish a clear, unanimous line in the class struggle.

These changes proved their worth in the higher level of rehearsal and performance of Cardew's *Great Learning Paragraph 5* at Cecil Sharp House on 21 January 1972, and the premier performance in Britain of Christian Wolff's piece *Burdocks* also at Cecil Sharp House on 28 March. However, these were pieces written for the 'old' Scratch Orchestra. When it came to our first composition for the 'new' Orchestra – the performance of two versions of a scene from *Sweet F.A.* (15) in combined opera-ballet form at the Bluecoat Hall concert in Liverpool on 26 January 1972, which depicted the struggle and triumph of a group of revolutionaries over a crowd of hippy students (loosely based on real events during the Newcastle tour) then we have to confess a musical failure. But it was only the first effort, and the 'Communists', far from being discouraged, have resolved to learn the lessons of the experience. We over-reached ourselves. Our first task was to learn from the people, then try out composition and performance, constantly testing theory against practice, returning again to the theory, thus progressing from small experiments eventually to real work for the proletariat, as the general level of political understanding, revolutionary solidarity, and the necessary musical skills are raised, step by step.

So this third phase, from July 1971 up to the time of writing May 1972, has been hesitant at times, but positive steps have been made, which show that the Scratch Orchestra is undergoing a qualitative change, after the quantitative accumulation of two years' experience, during which the contradictions within the Orchestra (also in the capitalist world in general) have matured and sharpened. We are undergoing an evolution from a lower to a higher stage of development. As a whole the period shows :

1) That the Scratch Orchestra has not broken up as people might have feared at the time of the Discontents. The established network of friendships, based on mutual respect, seems strong enough to weather the storms of the process of change.

2) That, under the impact of the Ideology Group, the Scratch Orchestra is capable of increasing its level of musical ability and performance potential – of improvement – through perseverance in rehearsal that was rarely seen before. The Scratch Orchestra has taken on a new lease of life. Members glimpse a future ahead with a sense of direction.

3) That, since all factions are stimulating each other to higher levels of performance, the Scratch Orchestra is now turning its attention to the interest of the audience.

4) But that we have much still to learn before we can solve the question of the audience, and how to serve the struggle of the oppressed working class. To learn more, with each public appearance we now programme time for discussion with the audience during concerts (so far with mixed and limited results, but at least a step in the right direction).

5) That Cardew's idea that the Scratch Orchestra should establish working relations with the class of working, professional musicians (some were brought in to participate in *Paragraph 5* and *Burdocks*) is good, since it stimulates the Orchestra to raise its own technical standards, and is a direct point of contact with working musicians in our society.

With the lessons of our past development in mind the Scratch Orchestra can begin to lay plans, and progress towards the future with hope. It must develop solidarity with the revolutionary class – the working class – in the only way possible, by joining them. That would be a noble contribution to the struggle, and the final march to victory over the decaying fascist system of monopoly capitalism.

'Finally, in times when the class struggle nears the decisive hour, the process of dissolution going on within the ruling class, in fact within the whole range of old society, assumes such a violent, glaring character, that a small section of the ruling class cuts itself adrift, and joins the revolutionary class, the class that holds the future in its hands. Just as, therefore, at an earlier period, a section of the nobility went over to the bourgeoisie, so now a portion of the bourgeoisie goes over to the proletariat, and in particular, a portion of the bourgeois ideologists, who have raised themselves to the level of comprehending theoretically the historical movement as a whole.' KARL MARX and FRIEDERICH ENGELS, *Communist Manifesto*, 1848.

The message of the times is clear. What is our role?

'Proletarian literature and art are part of the whole proletarian cause; they are, as Lenin said, cogs and wheels in the whole revolutionary machine.' MAO TSETUNG, *Talks at the Yenan Forum on Literature and Art*, 1942.

SMASH THE DECAYING IDEOLOGICAL AND CULTURAL SUPERSTRUCTURE!

SMASH THE BOURGEOIS CLASS AND ITS CORRUPT CAPITALIST SYSTEM!

DOWN WITH IMPERIALISM!

CHAPTER 2

Criticising Cage and Stockhausen

The American composer and writer John Cage, born 1912, and the German composer Karlheinz Stockhausen, born 1928, have emerged as the leading figures of the bourgeois musical avantgarde. They are ripe for criticism. The grounds for launching an attack against them are twofold: first, to isolate them from their respective schools and thus release a number of younger composers from their domination and encourage these to turn their attention to the problems of serving the working people, and second, to puncture the illusion that the bourgeoisie is still capable of producing 'geniuses'. The bourgeois ideologist today can only earn the title 'genius' by going to extreme lengths of intellectual corruption and dishonesty and this is just what Cage and Stockhausen have done. Inevitably, they try and lead their 'schools' along the same path. These are ample grounds for attacking them; it is quite wrong to think that such artists with their elite audiences are 'not doing anyone any harm'.

When the attack was launched it had the advantage of surprise. In my early career as a bourgeois composer I had been part of the 'school of Stockhausen' from about 1956–60, working as Stockhausen's assistant and collaborating with him on a giant choral and orchestral work. From 1958–68 I was also part of the 'school of Cage' and throughout the sixties I had energetically propagated, through broadcasts, concerts and articles in the press, the work of both composers. This was a bad thing and I will not offer excuses for it, but it certainly contributed to our 'advantage of surprise'. In 1972 Hans Keller of the BBC Music Section, knowing the history of my association with Cage, asked me to write an article in The Listener *to prepare the public for some Cage performances planned for the summer. The result must have surprised him, but it seems also to have pleased him, for shortly afterwards he asked me for an introductory talk to a broadcast of Stockhausen's* Refrain.

Bourgeois intellectual life is characterised by constant rivalry. The exponents of different schools are uninterruptedly cutting each other's throats and striving for advantage in all kinds of underhand ways, including the formation of temporary alliances. Thus the academic composers feel threatened by the avant-gardists, for example, fearing for their entrenched positions – but later you'll find them fraternising on some international panel, uniting to hold down some particularly promising upstart. Progressive intellectuals have to learn how to take advantage of such contradictions and use them. The Cage and Stockhausen articles were my first lesson and I made mistakes, with the result that I temporarily lost my voice at the BBC – my next talk On Criticism *was neither broadcast nor printed. Punishments were also meted out inside the BBC on account of the Stockhausen broadcast which by mischance was heard by a high official of the Corporation.*

There are probably errors in the articles on Cage and Stockhausen, but I have left them as they were, adding footnotes where necessary. The version of the Cage article printed here is the first draft, which was considerably shortened for publication in The Listener.

JOHN CAGE; GHOST OR MONSTER?

'MY MIND SEEMS IN SOME RESPECT LACKING SO THAT I MAKE OBVIOUSLY STUPID MOVES. I DO NOT FOR A MOMENT DOUBT THAT THIS LACK OF INTELLIGENCE AFFECTS MY MUSIC AND THINKING GENERALLY. HOWEVER, I HAVE A REDEEMING QUALITY: I WAS GIFTED WITH A SUNNY DISPOSITION.'
(Cage 1968)

Some years ago I received through the letterbox, as a free supplement with my regular copy of *China Pictorial*. Mao Tsetung's *Talks at the Yenan Forum on Literature and Art*. The *Talks*

34

were written in 1942 (16). In a recent edition I notice the Chinese commentator says 'The *Talks* are a magic mirror for detecting the ghosts and monsters in our theatres' (with reference to the bloodcurdling apparitions that were apparently a feature of traditional Chinese theatre) (17). It is a healthy exercise to hold up such a mirror to one's own work and the works of those one greatly respects or has greatly respected. Genuine criticism is motivated solely by the desire to strengthen what is good. Of course through strengthening what is good it will also contribute to the decline of what is not good, or no longer good. 'Good' is here understood to refer to everything that contributes towards social change in the desired direction, i.e. towards socialism.

'The first problem is: Literature and art for whom?' (*Talks*). Whom does Cage's music serve? We can answer this quite simply by looking at the audience, by seeing who supports this music and who attacks it. Ten years ago Cage concerts were often disrupted by angry music-lovers and argumentative critics. It was the most bourgeois elements in the audience that protested against it. But they soon learned to take their medicine. Nowadays a Cage concert can be quite a society event. The audience has grown and its class character has become clearer in proportion. What happens nowadays is that revolutionary students boycott Cage's concerts at American universities, informing those entering the concert hall of the complete irrelevance of the music to the various liberation struggles raging in the world (18). And if it does not support those struggles, then it is opposing them and serving the cause of exploitation and oppression. There is no middle course. 'There is no such thing as Art for Art's Sake, art that stands above classes, art that is detached from or independent of politics' (*Talks*).

'Works of art as ideological forms are products of the reflection in the human brain of the life of a given society.' (*Talks*). What aspects of present-day society are reflected in the work of John Cage? Randomness is glorified as a multicoloured kaleidoscope of perceptions to which we are 'omniattentive'. Like the 'action' paintings of Jackson Pollock, Cage's music presents the surface dynamism of modern society; he ignores the underlying tensions and contradictions that produce that surface (he follows McLuhan in seeing it as a manifestation of our newly

35

acquired 'electronic consciousness'). He does not represent it as an oppressive chaos resulting from the lack of planning that is characteristic of the capitalist system in decay (a riot of greed and exploitation). However, if progressive people begin to appreciate the music as reflecting this situation in fact, then it will become identified with everything we are fighting against.

Many younger composers and artists have been deeply affected by Cage's work at one stage or another (and I include myself in this category) and he has become a father figure to a number of superficially rebellious movements in the arts. In the '30s and '40s his work was hard-hitting and realistic, but what is he writing now?

Cheap Imitation (1970) is based on a work by Satie. The rhythm of the original is retained, the notes are changed. Cage here contradicts the interdependence of all the aspects of a structure. Any content, as well as the dynamism that is characteristic of 'saying something', is automatically lost if one aspect of the language is systematically altered. But the resulting emptiness does not antagonise the bourgeois audience which is confident of its ability to cultivate a taste for virtually anything. The appreciation of emptiness in art fits well with imperialist dreams of a depopulated world. 'The most, the best, we can do, we believe (wanting to give evidence of love), is to get out of the way, leave space around whomever or whatever it is. But there is no space!' (Cage 1966)

Musicircus (1967) is a totally 'empty' composition – it contains no notations at all, except the demand that participants should regulate their activity according to a timetable which is not provided. By way of analogy I heard a lecturer recently describe the history of the Sarabande as follows: the Sarabande was originally a lively Spanish dance used by prostitutes to attract customers. It ended up in the French court as a slow, stately piece of music allowing for the most intricate and refined elaboration of the melodic line. Is the circus to go the same way? It used to be a many-sided spectacle and entertainment for the people, produced by itinerant bands of gypsies and 'other foreigners'. Much of this character is retained even in the modern commercial circuses, and they are still very much 'for the people'. But with Cage the circus becomes an 'environment' for the bewilderment and titillation of a cultured audience. Instead of a trained band of white horses with plumes on their heads, you may find a little string orchestra inaudibly playing Spohr in evening dress, while numerous other groups get on with their own things. Instead of the elaborate and highly decorated machinery of the fairground, you will find banks of TV tubes, amplifiers, modulators and 'spaghetti' of all kinds, ensuring that in the event of anyone wishing to say something coherent they will be totally inaudible to the public.

'The life of the people is always a mine of the raw materials for literature and art, materials in their natural form, materials that may be crude, but are most vital, rich and fundamental.' (*Talks*). The Sarabande sacrificed its vitality on the altar of courtly culture and refinement. It looks as though Cage wants to dissipate the vitality of the circus into undifferentiated chaos and boredom.

Let's go back to *Variations I* (1958), which I regard as a key work in Cage's output. Unlike *Cheap Imitation*, the score of *Variations I* emphasises the total interdependence of all the attributes of a sound. Transparent sheets of lines and dots make up the score. The dots (sound events) are read in relation to a number of lines representing the various aspects of that sound: time of occurrence, loudness, duration, pitch, timbre. A change of position of a dot means a change in all the aspects of that sound event. Once Kurt Schwertsik (19) and I, overcome with Cage's 'beautiful idea' of letting sounds be sounds (and people be people, etc., etc., in other words seeing the world as a multiplicity of fragments without cohesion), decided to do a pure performance (no gimmicks) on horn and guitar, just reading the lines and dots and notating the results and letting the sounds be themselves. The result was a desert.

Contrary to his own 'beautiful idea', Cage himself, in his performance of this piece with David Tudor (20) never let the sounds be just sounds. Their performances were full of crashes, bangs, radio music and speech, etc. No opportunity for including emotive material was lost. And musically they were right. Without the emotive sounds the long silences that are a feature of the piece in its later stages would have been deprived of their drama and the piece disintegrate into the driest dust (as Schwertsik and I found out by painful experience).

The one merit of such a purely formal score is that it releases the initiative of the performer – it gives him participation in the act of composition and hence a genuinely educative experience. In the balance on the other side is the total indifference (implicitly represented by such a formalistic score) to the seriousness of the world situation in which it occurs. Can that one merit tip the scales? No, it can't, not even with the sunniest disposition in the world.

'Contrary to his beautiful ideas . . .' With the publication of *Silence* (1961) the rot set in. Beautiful ideas are welcome in every stately and semi-detached home and Cage became a name in the ears of the reading public, the intelligentsia.

There is a contradiction between the toughness of Cage's music and the softness of his ideas. The toughest of Cage's pieces that I have heard is *Construction in Metal*, one of three 'constructions' written about 1940. 'Collective violence' could describe this music; it might possibly awaken a listener to the idea that liberation requires violence.

His next book *A Year from Monday* (1968) includes a 'Diary: How to improve the world (you'll only make matters worse)'. In the Preface he states that he is now less interested in music, more interested in 'revolution', and recommends anarchism. In other words: the toughness (the music) is losing, the softness (the corrupt ideology) is winning.

For instance (just two out of literally thousands of such examples): 'Difference between pennilessness now and pennilessness then: now we've got unquestioned credit' (Diary 1966). Who's we? John Cage and the Queen of England? It sounds as though Cage would say: Anyone can survive today provided they play the system, never mind how corrupt.

An earlier one: 'We are as free as birds. Only the birds aren't free. We are as committed as birds, and identically.' (*Lecture on Commitment*, 1961). One is tempted to joke back, 'How does he know?' and forget it. But this is dangerous and lazy. Cage is putting forward a poisonous line here: artists are on the same level as partridges on a game preserve (to take one of the more relevant of the available interpretations).

In the early 1960s, Cage's *Atlas Eclipticalis* was included in a concert at Lincoln Centre, New York, played by a conventional symphony orchestra. The parts for the musicians are again arrangements of dots and lines (this time traced from a star atlas) and every player has contact microphones attached to his intrument and an amplification system. The performance was a shambles and many of the musicians took advantage of the confusion to abuse the electronic equipment to such a degree that Christian Wolff (usually an even-tempered man) felt compelled to rush in amongst them and protest against the extensive 'damage to property'. Cage lamented afterwards to the effect that his music provided freedom – freedom to be noble, not to run amok.

I find it impossible to deplore the action of those orchestral musicians. Not that they took a 'principled stand' (I hope such stands may be taken in the future), but they gave spontaneous expression to the sharply antagonistic relationship between the avantgarde composer with all his electronic gadgetry and the working musician. There are many aspects to this contradiction, but beneath it all is class struggle.

Life offers many lessons. Mistakes may be turned to advantage. The important thing for us artists and intellectuals is to 'move our feet over to the side of the workers'. (*Talks*). In so doing we may lose that part of our artistry and our intellectuality that is orientated towards bourgeois society and this loss should be celebrated, not bemoaned. The New York musicians gave Cage a lesson when they disrupted *Atlas*. Cage could have studied the reasons for this action – instead he coldly condemned it. The revolutionary students boycotting Cage's college concerts say quite clearly 'Your music is not saying anything to the world's people, it speaks only to a tiny band, a social intellectual elite'. But Cage waffles on about the 'haves and the have nots' as though it was all a question of pocket money, and ignores the lesson.

How can a composer truly reflect society if he ignores the lessons of that society? If a composer cannot or refuses to come to terms with such problems then the matter should be thrown open to public criticism. The artist serves the community, not vice versa.

Through broadcasts and public concerts a number of Cage's recent works will be heard in England this summer. *HPSCHD* (for 7 harpsichords, 52 tracks of tape, and a whole lot of audible and visible extras) is due for performance on 13 August. I have been engaged to play one of the harpsichords. I've heard that

39

the part is complex and difficult, but I wasn't asked whether I could play the instrument – and I know why : because it makes not the slightest difference what I play, or how I play it or how I feel about it. On the same degrading terms many talented and intelligent people will participate in that concert. Basically – judging from comments on an earlier performance : 'It was ensured that no order can be perceived' (Ben Johnston); 'One of the great artistic environments of the decade' (Kostelanetz) – it will be a king-size electronic multi-media freak-out, and I don't recommend anyone to go to it.

People often speak of the 'dilemma of the bourgeois artist', as though he was trapped, paralysed, unable to act. This is not the case. Ghosts have some sort of dilemma; they can never be alive. Monsters have one; they can never be human. But I see no dilemma for Cage. It may not be all plain sailing, but there's no reason why he can't shuffle his feet over to the side of the people and learn to write music which will serve their struggles.

The Listener, 4.5.72

The performance of HPSCHD *mentioned in the preceding article also included the pianist John Tilbury, who had earned a reputation as a performer of bourgeois avantgarde music. Some time later his recording of Cage's* Music of Changes *was broadcast by the BBC and he was asked to contribute an introductory talk. My article had touched on a number of Cage's works without going into any one in detail; in his talk, Tilbury remedied this omission and on the basis of his thorough knowledge of the* Music of Changes *he criticised it in detail though not exhaustively. His talk is reprinted here in full.*

INTRODUCTION TO CAGE'S *Music of Changes*
by JOHN TILBURY

The preface to Deryck Cooke's book *The Language of Music* contains the following passage : 'At the present time, attempts to elucidate the "content" of music are felt to be misguided, to say the least; the writer on musical matters is expected to ignore or only hint at what the composer had to say, and to concentrate entirely on how he said it. Or to put it in the contemporary way, he is expected to concentrate entirely on the "form", which is not regarded as "saying" anything at all. Thus the two inseparable aspects of an expressive art are separated and one is utterly neglected – much to the detriment of our understanding of the other. Instead of responding to music as what it is – the expression of man's deepest self – we tend to regard it more and more as a purely decorative art; and by analysing the great works of musical expression purely as pieces of decoration, we misapprehend their true nature, purpose and value. By regarding form as an end in itself, instead of as a means of expression, we make evaluations of composers' achievements which are irrelevant and worthless.' (21)

Now it is just this question of content in music that I want to raise in relation to Cage's work. How, in fact, can we apprehend the true nature, purpose and value of the *Music of Changes*?

Let us begin with the facts of the piece. The *Music of Changes* was written in 1951 and is the embodiment, wholly or partially, in musical expression of Cage's view of the world. By that I mean that before Cage can function as a musican he has to live as a man, and not as abstract man, but historically as a real man in a particular society. In the *Music of Changes* Cage is saying something about the real world, secreted through the sounds and silences which constitute the piece. You will have the opportunity later of hearing these sounds, experiencing these silences (and thankfully there is no substitute for that), but what of their origin, what is the nature of the compositional process that orders them?

Well, in fact this process is somewhat complicated though it is certainly not mysterious, and Cage has described it in detail in his book *Silence*.

Essentially, the arrangement of the material was determined by chance operations, by the tossing of coins. Charts of sounds, silences, amplitudes, durations were arranged so that they could interpret as musical material the coin oracle of the Chinese *Book of Changes*, so that they could accommodate a chance method of procedure. However, readings of the charts always encompassed, for example, all twelve notes of the chromatic scale so that the effect of the chance operations (the tossing of coins) was balanced to a certain extent by the composer's initial choice of materials (22). Technically, the result of Cage's application of

41

this method is brilliant – the way in which the piano is used as a sound source to be explored rather than an instrument to be played, the extensive use of the third sustaining pedal to achieve a wide range of colours and textures, the subtly changing resonances obtained, the overall pianistic clarity; and artistically, the effect is of stylistic coherence and originality.

But this is not all – in fact it is only half the story. For there is no such thing as an artistic conscience which is not governed by world outlook. In a class society such as our own an artist observes, selects, refines, in short, creates not simply according to his own needs, but, more importantly, to the needs of a particular class – the musical ideas which created the *Music of Changes* are necessarily ideologically rooted and it is only within the context of ideology that the question of the true nature of a work of art can be meaningfully answered.

Ironically, in spite of Cage's professed desire to strip his work of subjectivity, to free it of emotional content, individual taste, tradition, etc., ideas and concepts, Cage's ideas and concepts, are expressed *quite explicitly* in the *Music of Changes* and you don't have to read Cage's writings (illuminating as they are) to grasp its ideological content. In particular, there are three aspects of Cage's thought which the *Music of Changes* draws the listeners' attention to.

First, there is his concept that sounds should be themselves, that they enter the time-space centred within themselves, that they should be free from other sounds, free from human desire, free of association, so that any relationship between sounds is quite fortuitous, i.e. unconscious (23).

This aesthetic inevitably requires a sympathetic attitude on the part of the performer. The American pianist, David Tudor, described it in a recent interview in *Music and Musicians*, 'I had to learn,' he says, 'how to cancel my consciousness of any previous moment in order to produce the next one, bringing about the freedom to do anything.' In other words, true consciousness is attained not by understanding one's historical crib, but by simply 'cancelling' it; not in order to understand the dialectical relationship between freedom and necessity, but in order to be free to do anything, presumably to anybody and for any reasons (24).

The *Music of Changes* in fact bears a strong resemblance to

capitalist society, as Cage envisaged it in 1951; that is, as simply
the sum total of its individual members who merely proceed on
their own way, according to their own dictates. Each particle
of this universe appears to be free and spontaneously self-moving,
corresponding to the free bourgeois producer as he imagines
himself to be; events consist of their collisions and are the product
of internal chance. However, a mysterious cosmic force holds all
those particles together in one system; this mysterious force is
simply the capitalist law of supply and demand (25).

The second aspect of Cage's thought that I want to mention
is this question of chance. The majority of Cage's works use
random procedures of one kind or another. Just as in capitalist
society, and for bourgeois ideology, it is the free market, the
iron law of supply and demand, which holds all the bourgeois
producers together, inexplicably and arbitrarily determines and
adjusts their relations to each other, and acts as the grand
unifying principle – so in the *Music of Changes* (and many other
of Cage's works) randomness, chance is exalted to become the
controlling factor, and just as capitalist social relations engender
wars, mass hunger, pollution, neuroses, so Cage himself has described the *Music of Changes* as 'an object more inhuman than
human, having the alarming aspect of Frankenstein's Monster.'
And try as he may, Cage can no more resolve the contradictions of contemporary composition than he can the contradictions
of contemporary capitalism. For to resolve a contradiction it is
necessary to grasp the laws of motion and change, and act in
accordance with them. This is something Cage is patently unable
or unwilling to do. Cage's attitude to change is the third aspect
of his theory that we find clearly expressed in the *Music
of Changes*. Cage has often said that he is interested in quantity,
not quality, and change in the *Music of Changes* is precisely
quantitative, accumulative change. Thus the sound material does
not develop and change according to its own inner contradictions, but according to phenomena and conditions outside itself.
In the *Music of Changes* a randomised compositional procedure
is imposed mechanically on the sound material; tones and
aggregates may be liquidated, or displaced to reappear at different
points along the continuity in varying degrees of recognisability.
This mechanistic thinking also explains Cage's obsession with
technology. Thus, for him, the introduction of a new technique

from without can resolve contradictions (i.e. effect radical change) within, so that, for example, the contradiction of capitalism can be resolved by our newly-acquired, T.V. – inspired, electronic consciousness. Cage postulates unconscious individual participation as opposed to conscious class struggle. What is crucial is that Cage totally ignores the revolutionary aspect of change, change in quality based on the development of internal contradictions. The revolutionary aspirations which Cage professes flake away under scrutiny to reveal a deep-rooted, pie-in-the-sky liberalism.

What I have tried to show, briefly and incompletely, is that the true nature of a piece of music, like any work of art, is inextricably bound up with the ideological stand or world outlook of its creator, and that the content of a piece of music is not something mysterious, unattainable or elusive. On the contrary, creative listening, that is, listening to music that involves the mind as well as the ears and heart, can attain a measure of understanding of what a composer is saying about the world.

In the passage I quoted at the beginning of the talk Deryck Cooke also brought up the question of the purpose and value of works of art. The purpose of a work derives from its nature and is inseparable from it; furthermore, the purpose of a work, objectively, can be at variance with the subjective intentions of the composer (26).

The purpose of the *Music of Changes* is to propagate a world view, more specifically to universalise a bourgeois class view (i.e. the dilemma of this particular ruling class is presented as the dilemma of the human race as a whole, as the human condition in general), its purpose is to obscure the laws of motion and change and thereby to attempt to help stave off revolutionary change.

In the *Talks at the Yenan Forum on Literature and Art* Mao Tsetung wrote, 'A common characteristic of the literature and art of all exploiting classes in their period of decline is the contradiction between their reactionary political content and their artistic form.' The *Music of Changes* exemplifies this thesis perfectly; a pianistic masterpiece rooted in bourgeois individualism, anarchism and reformism. And what is its value? To the working and oppressed people it has no value, it bears no relation to their life. Its value is to the ruling class, it serves the stability of that class and is a weapon in their fight against revolution. Its value, therefore, is its counter-revolutionary value to the status quo, to imperialism; this, in the last analysis, is its true nature.

Cage serves imperialism and will go under with imperialism. But is it true to say that his music bears no relation to the lives of the working and oppressed people? In a way such music does reflect the conditions under which people work, with the productive forces catastrophically out of step with the relations of production, and in doing so it intensifies our oppression. It is certainly true that it can have no positive value to the working class; workers would have no difficulty in identifying the Music of Changes *as yet another horrible aspect of their oppressive environment – and they would not spend time going into just which characteristics of capitalism are peeking out at them through these calculated sounds and silences. But progressive artists have to settle accounts with their opposite numbers in the bourgeois camp, and there are some points outstanding.*

Tilbury talks about three particular 'aspects of Cage's thought' that this piece draws attention to. Rather does it reflect (draw attention to) three aspects of capitalist society, and three aspects of bourgeois ideology designed to mystify these aspects. The 'just sounds' idea reflects the conception of things as being isolated from one another, hence there is no point in investigating their interrelations, and if nobody investigates the relationships between things then the bourgeoisie will be able to maintain its rule. The 'randomness' idea is a familiar weapon of the bourgeois ideologists to divert the consciousness of the masses from the real laws (laws and randomness are counterposed) underlying the development of the world and human society. On the idea of 'quantitative change', Tilbury rightly points out that it denies the revolutionary aspect of change, even though Cage is constantly talking about 'revolution'. Thus we see that these are not just aspects of Cage's thought, but that Cage is propagating the main lines of the bourgeois ideological establishment. On the perceptual level his music may sound strange, but essentially he is singing the same old song.

So the Music of Changes *does not 'resemble' capitalist society 'as Cage envisaged it' (Tilbury). Cage, claiming mental incapacity, has never given serious thought to capitalist society. What he does is to reflect capitalist society and the mess it's in, and he reflects this mess in the very way the bourgeoisie would like it to be seen, as something that is not their responsibility. Cage's music is in fact a much more genuine reflection of the straits of the present-day bourgeoisie than are the blue movies or Wagner operas that the bourgeoisie undoubtedly prefers for its cultural recreation. Cage at least tries to reproduce the world (the bourgeois world) and not the kingdom of heaven, as does Stockhausen. The aspect of Cage that engages our fury is his denial of the conscious role of the individual, of responsibility; in denying this, he is guilty of a vicious deception. No art drops from the sky; all art bears the imprint of the real world, even if its only reality is that it reproduces a lie being put about by the bourgeoisie. The area of criticism of the individual artist is the area of his conscious participation as an individual: what does he choose to reflect, for whom, from which class standpoint, and what intellectual and emotional penetration does he bring to it?*

This raises problems that are not easy to deal with (and I don't propose to deal with them here), such as the degree of freedom of choice available to the bourgeois composer, especially the nameless one who does not aspire to the influential position of a Cage or a Stockhausen. One thing is sure; discussion of these problems can in no way undercut the rightness of criticising Cage and Stockhausen, who have voluntarily come forward to take up the role of leading ideologists for the bourgeoisie on the artistic front. The articles above and the talk on Stockhausen that follows depict this servile role quite starkly and show it as an objective fact, whatever protestations the composers themselves may make to the contrary.

STOCKHAUSEN SERVES IMPERIALISM

This talk has taken a different shape from the one I originally planned. I had meant to go into the development of the avant-garde in Germany through the Nazi regime and after the war through the Darmstadt School (27). However, I soon experienced a real dislike for contributing to the already proliferous documentation of the avantgarde. I decided to tackle the subject from a wider viewpoint.

Stockhausen's *Refrain*, the piece I have been asked to talk about, is a part of the cultural superstructure of the largest-scale system of human oppression and exploitation the world has ever known : imperialism. The way to attacking the heart of that system is through attacking the manifestations of that system, not only the emanations from the American war machine in Vietnam, not only the emanations from Stockhausen's mind, but also the manifestations of this system in our own minds, as deep-rooted wrong ideas. And we must attack them not only on the superficial level, as physical cruelty or artistic nonsense or muddled thinking, but also on the fundamental level for what they are : manifestations of imperialism.

My saying something doesn't necessarily make it true. The task of this article is to make clear that Stockhausen's *Refrain* is in fact – not just in my opinion – a part of the cultural superstructure of imperialism. The task falls into three parts. To expose the essential character of the musical avantgarde in general; to outline the particular development of the avantgarde in which Stockhausen plays a role; and to indicate the position and content of *Refrain* within that development.

The avantgarde period (consisting of successive avantgardes) is not the latest, but the last chapter in the history of bourgeois music. The bourgeois class audience turns away from the contemporary musical expression of its death agony, and contemporary bourgeois music becomes the concern of a tiny clique taking a morbid interest in the process of decay. I must avoid giving the impression that this tiny clique of the avantgarde has its own kind of purity and honesty in representing the collapse of imperialism and bourgeois values in general. No, imperialism is rotten to the core and so is its culture. However, the ruling classes – the big business men, the politicians, the field marshals, the media controllers, etc. – don't just 'turn away' to groan and expire gracefully. They fight to stave off their collapse and in this fight they use all the means at their disposal – economic, military, political, cultural, ideological. The aim of the establishment is to use ideas not as a liberating force for clarification and enlightenment and the releasing of people's initiative, but as an enslaving

47

force, for confusion and deception and the perversion of talent. In this way they hope to stave off collapse.

There has always been a mass of talent in the avantgarde and some of this talent is keen to leave the restricted world of the avantgarde and its preoccupations behind and take up a more definite role in the service of imperialism, a role with a larger following and bigger rewards. In 1959, the year he wrote *Refrain*, Stockhausen was ripe for this role. At that time he was a leading figure in the Darmstadt School which had been set up after the Second World War to propagate the music and ideas that the Nazis had banished. The Nazis branded the avantgarde 'degenerate' and publicly disgraced it and suppressed it. In postwar Germany a subtler technique was used; instead of suppression, repressive tolerance. The European avantgarde found a nucleus in Darmstadt where its abstruse, pseudo-scientific tendencies were encouraged in ivory tower conditions. By 1959 it was ready to crack from its own internal contradictions and the leading figures were experiencing keenly the need for a broader audience. For this the music had to change. *Refrain* was probably the first manifestation of this change in Stockhausen's work. Since then his work has become quite clearly mystical in character. In a recent interview he says that a musician when he walks on stage 'should give that fabulous impression of a man who is doing a sacred service' (note the showmanship underlying that remark). He sees his social function as bringing an 'atmosphere of peaceful spiritual work to a society that is under so much strain from technical and commercial forces'.

In *Refrain* we can see the beginnings of the tendencies that his present music exhibits alongside the remains of his Darmstadt work.

The score itself is a gimmick typical of Darmstadt thinking. The music is obliged quite mechanically to accommodate itself to a crude piece of mobile two-dimensional design. It is written on a large card with music staves that bow into partial circles centred on the middle of the card. Anchored to this middle point is a strip of transparent plastic with some notations on it. These notations are the recurring refrain that gives the piece its title.

The instrumentation is piano, vibraphone, celeste, each of the three players also using auxiliary instruments as well as vocal exclamations and tongue clicks. Visualising the kind of musicians

48

required for this, we see the beginnings of the specially trained band of players that are necessary for the presentation of his recent work.

The performance itself creates a situation of intense concentration and listening for the musicians. This listening activity of the musicians communicates itself to the audience and it is this intense concentration and contemplation of sounds for their own sake that reveals the beginnings of the mystical atmosphere that Stockhausen has cultivated more and more theatrically since then.

Some may criticise Stockhausen on the grounds that he presents mystical ideas in a debased and vulgar form. This is true, but it is not enough. To attack debasement and vulgarity in themselves is meaningless. We have to penetrate the nature of the ideas that are being debased and vulgarised and if they are reactionary, attack *them*. What is this mysticism that is being peddled in a thousand guises, lofty and debased, throughout the imperialist world? Throughout its long history in India and the Far East, mysticism has been used as a tool for the suppression of the masses. Salesmen like Stockhausen would have you believe that slipping off into cosmic consciousness removes you from the reach of the painful contradictions that surround you in the real world. At bottom, the mystical idea is that the world is illusion, just an idea inside out heads. Then are the millions of oppressed and exploited people throughout the world just another aspect of that illusion in our minds? No, they aren't. The world is real, and so are the people, and they are struggling towards a momentous revolutionary change. Mysticism says 'everything that lives is holy', so don't walk on the grass and above all don't harm a hair on the head of an imperialist. It omits to mention that the cells on our bodies are dying daily, that life cannot flourish without death, that holiness disintegrates and vanishes with no trace when it is profaned, and that imperialism has to die so that the people can live.

Well, that's about all I wish to say about *Refrain*. To go into it in greater detail would simply invest the work with an importance that it doesn't have. No, my job is not to 'sell' you *Refrain*. I see my job as raising the level of consciousness in regard to cultural affairs.

At the outset I said *Refrain* is part of the cultural superstructure of imperialism. These terms: 'superstructure', 'imperialism', require some explanation if the level of consciousness with regard to cultural affairs is to be raised, if we want to grasp the deeper roots of such surface phenomena as avantgarde music. These terms are essential to Marxism, and yet a lot of people seem to regard them as some sort of jargon or mumbo-jumbo. The truth is that in an imperialist country like Britain it would be a miracle indeed to find Marxism being taught in schools, since Marxism is directed towards the overthrow of imperialism, whereas the education system of an imperialist country must be directed towards maintaining imperialism. It is as well to bear this hard fact in mind.

In Marx's analysis, society consists of an economic base, and rising above this foundation, and determined by it, a superstructure of laws, politics, ideas and customs. The following quotation is to be found in Lenin's pamphlet entitled *Karl Marx*, which I have found the most concise and useful introduction to Marxism. Marx writes:

'In the social production of their life, men enter into definite relations that are indispensable and independent of their will, relations of production which correspond to a definite stage of development of their material productive forces. The sum total of these relations of production constitutes the economic structure of society, the real foundation, on which rises a legal and political superstructure and to which correspond definite forms of social consciousness. The mode of production of material life conditions the social, political and intellectual life process in general. It is not the consciousness of men that determines their being, but, on the contrary, their social being that determines their consciousness. At a certain stage of their development, the material productive forces of society come in conflict with the existing relations of production, or – what is but a legal expression for the same thing – with the property relations within which they have been at work hitherto. From being forms of development of the productive forces these relations turn into their fetters. Then begins an epoch of social revolution. With the change of the economic foundation the entire immense superstructure is more or less rapidly transformed. In considering such transformations a distinction should always be made between the material transformation of the economic conditions of production, which can be determined with the precision of natural science, and the legal, political, religious, aesthetic or philosophic – in short, ideological forms in which men become conscious of this conflict and fight it out.' (28)

Marx lived in the age of the development of capitalism. He describes the development towards monopoly capitalism, which he calls 'the immanent law of capitalistic production itself, the centralisation of capital'. He says :

'One capitalist always kills many. Hand in hand with this centralisation, or this expropriation of many capitalists by few, develop, on an ever-extending scale, the co-operative form of the labour process, the conscious technical application of science, the methodical cultivation of the soil, the transformation of the instruments of labour into instruments of labour only usable in common, the economising of all means of production by their use as the means of production of combined, socialised labour, the entanglement of all peoples in the net of the world market, and with this, the international character of the capitalistic regime. Along with the constantly diminishing number of the magnates of capital, who usurp and monopolise all advantages of this process of transformation, grows the mass of misery, oppression, slavery, degradation, exploitation; but with this too grows the revolt of the working class, a class always increasing in numbers, and disciplined, united, organised by the very mechanism of the process of capitalist production itself. The monopoly of capital becomes a fetter upon the mode of production, which has sprung up and flourished along with, and under it. Centralisation of the means of production and socialisation of labour at last reach a point where they become incompatible with their capitalist integument. This integument is burst asunder.' (29)

Marx, who died in 1883, did not live to see the imperialist wars of this century. It fell to Lenin to describe the development of imperialism in his pamphlet *Imperialism, the highest stage of capitalism* which he wrote in 1917. Here is what he says, with some omissions for the sake of brevity :

'Imperialism emerged as the development and direct continuation of the fundamental characteristics of capitalism in general. But capitalism only became capitalist imperialism at a definite and very high stage of its development, when certain of its fundamental characteristics began to change into their opposites . . .

Free competition is the fundamental characteristic of capitalism, and of commodity production generally; monopoly is the exact opposite of free competition, but we have seen the latter being transformed into monopoly before our eyes . . . At the same time, the monopolies, which have grown out of free competition, do not eliminate the latter, but exist over it and alongside it, and thereby give rise to a number of very acute, intense antagonisms, frictions and conflicts. Monopoly is the transition from capitalism to a higher system . . . Imperialism is capitalism in that stage of development in which the dominance of monopolies and finance capital has established itself; in which the export of capital has acquired pronounced importance; in which the division of the world among the international trusts has begun; in which the division of all territories of the globe among the biggest capitalist powers has been completed.'

Lenin brings out the aggressive, militaristic, brutal character of imperialism in his 1920 preface to the pamphlet. He says :

'Capitalism has grown into a world system of colonial oppression and of the financial strangulation of the overwhelming majority of the population of the world by a handful of "advanced" countries. And this "booty" is shared between two or three powerful world marauders armed to the teeth (America, Great Britain, Japan), who involve the whole world in *their* war over the sharing of *their* booty.'

'One capitalist always kills many'. Marx here graphically indicates the ruthlessness of economic development. In the economic base this produces the contradiction between free competition (i.e. private enterprise) and monopoly capitalism. How does this contradiction manifest itself in the superstructure? It manifests itself in multitudinous ways, but I will talk only about its manifestation in the field of art.

Here I must pause briefly to explain the word 'bourgeois'. The bourgeois class is that which becomes dominant with the development of capitalism. It is the class that lives by employing the labour of others and deriving profit from it. Bourgeois culture is the culture of this class. Concurrent with the development of capitalistic private enterprise we see the corresponding development in bourgeois culture of the individual artistic genius. The genius is the characteristic product of bourgeois culture. And just as private enterprise declines in the face of monopolies, so the whole individualistic bourgeois world outlook declines and becomes degenerate, and the concept of genius with it. Today, in the period of the collapse of imperialism any pretensions to artistic genius are a sham.

Earlier I drew attention to the fact that the ruling classes fight tooth and nail to stave off collapse. What are their tactics on the cultural front, the musical front in particular? The attention of the general public must not be drawn to the cultural expression of the collapse of imperialism, namely the degenerate avantgarde. To actively suppress it *would* draw attention. We know that the Nazis' suppression of the avantgarde in fact gave the impetus for considerable developments of the avantgarde. So it is fostered as the concern of a tiny clique and thus prevented from doing any real damage to the ruling classes. In this tiny clique genius is still cultivated, especially when some composer (like Stockhausen or Cage) appears eager to propagate an ideological line – such as mysticism or anarchism or reformism – that is in so far friendly to imperialism in that it opposes socialism and the ideas that would contribute to the organisation of the working class for the overthrow of imperialism. So we see Stockhausen adopting all the hallmarks of the genius of popular legend : arrogance, intractability, irrationality, unconventional appearance, egomania.

But all this is a small-scale operation compared with the tactics of the ruling class against the direct class enemy, the working class. In this area we find tactics comparable to the 'saturation bombing' technique of the Americans in Vietnam. There are two main lines of attack. First wide-scale promotion of the image of bourgeois culture in its prime, the music of the classical and romantic composers (the whole education system is geared to this). Second, the promotion of mass-produced music for mass consumption. Besides bringing in enormous profits, their hope is that this derivative music (film music, pop music, musical comedy, etc.) (30) will serve for the ideological subjugation of the working class. Both these lines attempt to encourage working class opportunism. The first through a kind of advertising campaign : 'bourgeois is best', and the second through encouraging degenerate tendencies, drugs, mass hypnosis, sentimentality.

Lenin remarked that the English working class could never be kept under by force, only by deception. In other words, the ruling class maintains its domination over the working people by telling lies and distorting the truth. The purpose of ideological struggle is to expose these lies and distortions. You now have the opportunity to hear Stockhausen's *Refrain*. I've exposed the true character of the piece as part of the superstructure of imperialism. I've shown that it promotes a mystical world outlook which is an ally of imperialism and an enemy of the working and oppressed people of the world. If in the light of all this it still retains any shred of attractiveness, compare it with other manifestations of imperialism today : the British Army in Ireland, the mass of unemployed, for example. Here the brutal character of imperialism is evident. Any beauty that may be detected in *Refrain* is merely cosmetic, not even skin-deep.

You might ask : Should I now switch off and protect myself from such ideas by not listening? Well, yes, by all means, that wouldn't be a bad thing in itself. But in the general context these ideas are too widely promoted to be ignored. They must be confronted and their essence grasped. They must be subjected to fierce criticism and a resolute stand taken against them.

What was the effect of the campaign against Cage and Stockhausen? I received a number of letters in response to the broadcast of 'Stockhausen serves Imperialism', and the publication of the first half of this talk in The Listener *provoked a storm in its correspondence columns. Seven letters were printed, most of them heatedly defending Stockhausen and attacking my music – but not my criticism. A review by Keith Rowe criticising a concert and TV appearance by Cage from the same standpoint appeared in* Microphone *magazine in June 1972 and created an equivalent flurry of correspondence. This led the editor, while contemptuously dismissing Rowe's review, to propose an entire issue of the magazine devoted to the questions that had been raised.*

These flurries demonstrated that there was a great eagerness to discuss artistic questions from a political point of view. The contradictoriness of the response showed that there was widespread lack of clarity on the basic questions of aesthetics and politics and their interrelations. Objectively there existed and still exists a need and a demand amongst musicians and their audiences for clarity on the question of the criteria to be used in evaluating music.

It was a symptom of this need that Hans Keller organised two series of talks on the BBC entitled Composers on Criticism *and* Critics on Criticism. *Naturally, in putting out these series, the BBC had no intention of achieving clarity on the question: rather the opposite. Their technique was to set up a large number of individuals to give their opinions in separate broadcasts and not allow any discussions which might have led to the issues being sorted out. My proposal for such a discussion was rejected on the grounds that it would require too much work! My own contribution to the series, which was commissioned about the time of the Stockhausen talk, was rejected on the grounds that it was irrelevant!*

The real reason for its rejection was, of course, that it was in fact relevant: relevant to the need and demand for the sober critical atmosphere that I mentioned above. I used the rejected talk as a lecture on a number of occasions and the discussions that it provoked proved its relevance. Despite numerous imperfections, some of which are taken up in the notes, the talk is printed here in full in its original form. This brings the chapter on the criticism of Cage and Stockhausen to an end.

ON CRITICISM

To begin I'd like to read a quotation from John Cage.

'A most salient feature of contemporary art is the fact that each artist works as he sees fit, and not in accordance with widely-agreed-upon procedures. Whether this state of affairs pleases or displeases us is not exactly clear from a consideration of modern cliches of thought.

'On the one hand we lament what we call the gulf between artist and society, between artist and artist, and we praise (very much like children who can only window shop for candy they cannot buy) the unanimity of opinion out of which arose a Gothic cathedral, an opera by Mozart, a Balinese combination of music and dance. We lament the absence among us of such generally convincing works, and we say it must be because we have no traditional ways of making things. We admire from a lonely distance that art which is not private in character but is characteristic of a group of people and the fact that they were in agreement. On the other hand, we admire an artist for his originality and independence of thought, and we are displeased when he is too obviously imitative of another artist's work. In admiring originality, we feel quite at home. It is the one quality of art we feel fairly capable of obtaining. Therefore we say such things as : Everyone not only has but should have his own way of doing things. Art is an individual matter. We go so far as to give credence to the opinion that a special kind of art arises from a special neurosis pattern of a particular artist. At this point we grow slightly pale and stagger out of our studios to knock at the door of some neighbourhood psychoanalyst. Or – we stay at home, cherish our differences, and increase our sense of loneliness and dissatisfaction with contemporary art. In the field of music, we express this dissatisfaction variously : we say; The music is interesting, but I don't understand it. Somehow it is not fulfilled. It doesn't have "the long line". We then go our separate paths : some of us back to work to write music that few find any use for, and others to spend their lives with the music of another time which, putting it bluntly and chronologically, does not belong to them.' (31)

This is what John Cage wrote in 1948 at the age of 36. Substantially the same analysis could be made today, and substantially I agree with it. It is an expression of disillusion and frustration – the composer's bright dreams wither up and die for lack of audience – discontent with the state of music today as compared with the music of the past, which he says, revelling in his isolation, does not belong to us. Actually it does belong to us, to do with as we see fit. We must make the past serve the present. But I'll come back to this.

I believe I speak for the vast majority of music lovers when I say : let's face it, modern music (modern classical music as it is called) is not half as good as classical music (which includes baroque classical, classical classical and romantic classical music, etc.). What does 'good' mean in that sentence? It means effective, wholesome, moving, satisfying, delightful, inspiring, stimulating and a whole lot of other adjectives that are just as widely understood and acknowledged and just as hard to pin down with any precision. These are the judgements of the music-loving public. By comparison with the effectiveness, wholesomeness, emotion, satisfaction, delight, inspiration and stimulus that we (that is, classical music-lovers, and we are a class audience) (32) derive from Beethoven, Brahms and the rest, modern music (with very few exceptions) is footling, unwholesome, sensational, frustrating, offensive and depressing. Why is this? It is because the bourgeois/capitalist society that brought music out of church into the realm of bourgeois art, and reached undreamed-of power and imperial glory through the upheavals of the industrial revolution, and also undreamed-of power of artistic expression, is now in the last stages of decay, and modern music reflects that decay.

Because modern music is bad in this sense, decadent, it cannot submit itself to principled, objective criticism, it does not set up the criteria by which it would expose itself as nonsense.

I experienced this personally as a student at the Royal Academy of Music. The nearest we ever got to establishing a criterion was some remark like 'it has a good shape'. In fact, the handwriting, or the neatness of the layout of the score seemed to be a matter of more importance. There were some good sound practical considerations such as 'Can it be heard?' 'It looks interesting on paper, but what does it sound like?'

In retrospect I appreciate the technical criteria, dealing with the transformation of formal ideas into sound, even those to do with neat presentation, but the rest were so vague as to be useless. In fact I really can't remember what they were. I don't believe any criteria were applied.

The result was that when I came to occupy a teaching position myself at the Royal Academy of Music I instinctively took the line of 'no criticism'. Occasionally I might take issue with a technical point that seemed particularly crass, but generally as regards technical criticism I regarded it as secondary, and to apply secondary criteria while not applying the primary criteria would obviously result in misplaced emphasis.

Also in retrospect I realise that I am not at all qualified to apply technical criteria because in my own period of training I had never mastered anything more than the rudiments. The rest had seemed irrelevant in view of my desire to break with the traditions of tonal music completely. The fact that I was able to pass exams and get diplomas despite my extremely limited com-

57

positional technique is due entirely to the fatally liberalistic attitude that permeates our education system.

Liberalism is just as oppressive as the religious dogma of the nineteenth century that it replaces. Liberalism is a tactic whereby the sting is taken out of the huge contradictions that run right through our cultural environment, so that we are tempted to pass them over and ignore them.

If a rebellious composer has to confront the situation that he cannot graduate from the Royal Academy of Music, then his rebellion may be broken if it is insubstantial in the first place, but if it is not then it will be immeasurably strengthened and his rebellion will be directed consciously against the establishment. This is a confrontation that the establishment is anxious to avoid, hence its tactic of liberalism.

'No criticism' in a teaching situation leads to psychologically insupportable emphasis on 'self-criticism', resulting in introversion and lack of confidence. In 1969 Michael Parsons, Howard Skepton and I founded the Scratch Orchestra, a group of about fifty people devoted to experimental performance arts. Some were students, some office workers, some amateur musicians, some professional, and there were several composers. From the beginning our line was 'no criticism'.

The products of 'no criticism at all' are weak and watery; the products of 'no criticism except self-criticism' are intensely introverted. The tension built up until, after two years, the floodgates were opened and the members of the Scratch Orchestra poured out their discontent. This stage represents 'collective self-criticism' and from it emerged criteria that we could apply.

This collective self-criticism was fruitful not in terms of output – this decreased sharply – but in terms of the seriousness and commitment of the members. The collective self-criticism was also painful, and so the criteria that came out of it are the product of struggle in a human situation, not an abstract scaffolding erected for aspiring composers to hang their beautiful ideas on. Perhaps they are not even criteria, just questions whereby a composer can externalise his self-criticism and actually do something about it.

Firstly : what does a composer think he's doing? Why and in what spirit does he sit down to compose? Is it to express his inmost soul? Or to communicate his thoughts? Or to entertain

58

an audience? Or educate them? Or to get rich and famous? Or to serve the interests of the community and if so what community, what class?

Secondly : does the music fulfil the needs of the audience? This immediately opens up two areas of study. First the different audiences that exist, where they overlap and what their class character is. And second, what the needs of the different audiences are, what are their aspirations, what are their standards (which means what are their criteria for appreciating music), and are we content to accept these or must we progressively change them?

Thirdly : do the compositions adequately meet the demands of the musicians playing them? A composition should give the musicians involved a creative role in a collective context. If a composition doesn't create a stimulating situation for the musicians involved it is very unlikely that it will stimulate an audience except in a negative way.

Fourthly : what is the material of a composition? It's not just notes and rests, and it's not just a beautiful idea that originates in the unique mind of a genius. It's ideas derived from experience, from social relations, and what the composer does is to transform these ideas into configurations of sound that evoke a corresponding response in the listener.

Fifthly : what is the basis of a composer's economic survival in society? He can take employment in education, in the service of the state, teaching what he has learnt to other composers, or investigating the 'nature of music' (whatever that may be). Or he can take employment in industry, writing film or background music, or commercial music of other kinds. Or he can attempt to win the support of an audience. Or a combination of these.

I must say, as a student at the Royal Academy of Music it would have been extremely useful if these matters had been brought up for consideration, never mind how reluctant I might have appeared at the time to take any notice .

Now I should like to talk about music criticism as a profession. Much propaganda is being done for the view that people are motivated by self-interest, the desire for money or fame or both. This is not true. The majority of people have a definite need to feel that they are serving the community in some way. We need the feeling that we are performing a useful function in society and not just living off society or other individuals in a parasitic way. Most music critics feel the same need.

Critics are an important link in the complex network that constitutes the relations of production of the musical profession. What can they do to serve the community?

A couple of months ago I noticed Andrew Porter saying something just at the end of a review of Wagner's *Ring* in Glasgow about Wagner's dream of the eventual end of capitalism as represented in *Götterdämmerung*. (This was in the *Financial Times*.) I must say, this inspired my curiosity. I have never seen a Wagner opera, although I have seen Hollywood's *Magic Fire* based on his life. *Magic Fire* bears about as much relation to reality as a Tarzan story (33). I also know a piano duet version of the Prelude to Act III of *Tristan and Isolde*, and once played in the fifth desk of cellos in a non-professional performance of the same piece. As regards Wagner's life I know that he was exiled from Germany for his part in a people's uprising in 1849 (34), the same year Karl Marx was exiled (35). This is the sum total of my knowledge about the most controversial composer of the nineteenth century. I can hear someone saying, 'My lad, if you've reached the ripe age of 36 without having learnt anything about Wagner, you have only yourself to blame.' Well, I think the reason is different. The reason is that virtually everything written and said about Wagner and his music is extremely boring and irrelevant to the present time, and reasonable musicians with a certain amount of work to do could not be expected to plough through it.

What does Wagner's music mean in relation to present-day society? If he had theories of Utopian socialism then it would be good to hear about them and criticise them. What is the historical basis of the myths that provide the material for the *Ring*? It would be wonderful to open a daily newspaper and find material of this kind, instead of yet another series of opinions and comments on performances, interpretations, readings of the score, etc. The music critic should indicate the cultural and political context of a work, and point out how the work relates to it and what relevance these matters have to society today.

With regard to the work of living composers the critic's task is exceptionally important. On the one hand he is the spokesman of the people. He must demand works that relate directly to the issues and struggles and preoccupations of the present, and lead the way forward to a better society, a truly socialist society. And on the other hand he must stringently criticise such works from the point of view of both form and content, with the aim of building up their strength. He should do this conscientiously and thoroughly, so that strong links will be forged between composers and critics, so that composers and critics can feel united in the performance of a common task in the service of the community, namely the production of good music for the benefit of the people.

'Good music'? According to what criteria is it 'good'? And a basic criterion has already been implied, the criterion of the 'people's benefit'.

On the simplest level we can say any music is good that benefits the people, any music is bad that harms them, that tends in the long run to make their conditions of existence worse than they are now or the same as they are now. To make things stay the same is possibly the most grievous harm imaginable. This is the criterion of the people's benefit.

Then: by what criterion do people judge their conditions of existence to be better or worse? (Basically this is the same criterion that composers and critics apply to their work, because composers and critics are people too, with a productive social role like other workers.) Good conditions of existence are: when your needs, physical and spiritual, are fulfilled, when you are conscious of the way your work, your productive activity, contributes to the society you live in, and when – through this consciousness and because your needs are not frustrated – you are able to expand and develop your work so as to maximise its usefulness to society.

So the 'people's good' is this: their basic needs are satisfied, and they are conscious of their position in society; when these two conditions are met, the people's creative energy is released, they can contribute to changing the world. Everything benefits the people that (a) satisfies their needs, (b) raises their level of consciousness, and (c) (following from the others) encourages them to develop the energy and ability and initiative to change the world according to their collective needs. This is socialist construction.

Is capitalist society as we know it today orientated towards benefiting the people? Let's apply the criteria. Does capitalism satisfy the people's needs? No, it regards the people as consumers, (36) and floods them with plastic bottles and white bread which bring vast profits to the manufacturers but no benefit to the consumers, so that the majority of people remain in conditions of hardship while the ruling class and its hangers-on live more and more luxuriously and more and more wastefully. Does capitalism raise the people's level of consciousness? No, the mass media feed lies to the people (as, for instance, saying that the miners in their strike were holding the nation up for ransom, whereas in fact they were not striking at the 'nation' but at the government and the ruling class), it feeds them platitudes under the guise of education, and crime and violence and sentimentality under the guise of entertainment. No, the mass media not only don't raise the level of consciousness of the people, they try to lower it, they aim to deceive the people.

Obviously these two negatives – not satisfying the people's needs and not raising their level of consciousness – do not produce a positive. In fact under capitalism today people are not encouraged to develop the energy, ability and initiative to change the world according to their collective needs. There is no such thing as socialist construction under capitalism, though Labour politicans will go on asserting that there is until they are blue in the face. There can only be socialist construction in opposition to capitalism (37).

I have been talking about politics. It's evident that the criterion of 'the people's good' is a political criterion. In music, the criterion 'good music is that which benefits the people' is a political criterion. 'Raising the level of consciousness of the people' is a political task. Everything that music can do towards raising the level of consciousness of the people is part of this political task, it subserves this political task. The artist cannot ignore politics. As Mao Tsetung says, 'There is no such thing as art that is detached from or independent of politics.' And I think I have also made clear what he means in the sentence, 'Each class in every class society has its own political and artistic criteria, but all classes in all class societies put the political criterion first and the artistic

62

criterion second.' This is profoundly true, this point about the precedence of political criteria over artistic criteria. It can be seen to be true, objectively, in capitalist society and it will still be true in a socialist society (38). To deny this is to cast yourself adrift in the realm of fantasy and, if you are an artist, your work will still be judged according to the political criterion first and the artistic criterion second and it will be seen – notwithstanding any artistic merit it may have – to be misleading the people, not raising their level of consciousness, and hence supporting capitalism and serving to prolong its domination of the working and oppressed people.

CHAPTER 3

A Critical Concert

I spent the year 1973 in West Berlin as a guest of the DAAD (German Academic Exchange Service) 'Berlin Artists Programme'. Every year this programme invites thirty or so artists from all over the world to live in Berlin and 'contribute to the cultural life of the city'. The people of Berlin and in particular the working people show a marked lack of enthusiasm for the contributions of these artists, and the German artists living in Berlin are also justifiably irritated by this importation of a highly-paid elite from abroad to divide their ranks and cream off the juiciest commissions. Karl Ruhrberg, who was running the programme while I was there, claims to have been 'helping artists' for twenty-five years. Speaking to some of the artists he is supposed to have helped one receives a very different impression. Guests of the Berlin Artists Programme face a number of unacceptable alternatives when they arrive in Berlin: a frustrating battle to impose their work on an unwelcoming community; loneliness and isolation if they are unwilling or unable to do this; opting out by calling in at Berlin only to receive their cheques, and spending the rest of the time globe-trotting or in their native countries; or servilely collaborating with the Programme and accepting the degenerate social round of cocktail parties and receptions. Some of the artists use their well-paid year as a kind of initial capital investment to build themselves an art career in Berlin, and continue to base themselves there afterwards. Others, who may accept the engagement because they are in financial straits, return home afterwards to find their economic outlook as bleak or bleaker than when they left.

One of the channels through which the musician 'guests' ('prisoners' would be more appropriate) of the Programme can present their work to the public is 'Musikprojekte', a concert series organised by the Berlin composer Erhard Grosskopf. Grosskopf, despite the economic discrepancy between him and the well-paid guest composers, realises the necessity of uniting where possible with the visitors on the basis of opposition to the cultural oppression of capitalist society. Grosskopf engaged me to present a concert at the Academy of Arts on 7 April 1973. I decided to present Christian Wolff's Accompaniments *and Frederic Rzewski's compositions* Coming Together *and* Attica. *These two American composers had both been aware of the development of the Scratch Orchestra (in fact, works of theirs had featured prominently in the early repertoire of the orchestra), and had also followed the process of its struggle and transformation with interest. The new work* Accompaniments *had been rejected for performance by the Scratch Orchestra in December 1972.* Coming Together *and* Attica *had already been heard in Berlin the previous summer, and had even generated a certain amount of enthusiasm. However, both these composers were presenting political themes and it was timely to submit their works to a critical appraisal in a public concert. The form of the concert was as follows; first the compositions were played (Wolff's first, then Rzewski's), then I gave a short talk and led a discussion with the audience. To create conditions for the discussion, a programme book was printed which included, besides elementary programme material about the compositions (texts and composers' notes), a draft of my introductory talk and reprints of 'Stockhausen Serves Imperialism' and Tilbury's 'Introduction to Cage's Music of Changes'. The line that we intended to pursue in the discussion was thus clearly stated.*

For the present purpose I have rearranged the material slightly and added a 'report' written shortly after the concert. The programme material on the compositions is sandwiched between the Introductory Talk and the Report.

INTRODUCTORY TALK FOR DISCUSSION AT WOLFF/ RZEWSKI CONCERT

Nobody imagines we live in the 'best of all possible worlds'. In our personal relationships, our work, in our cultural activity, in everything we do we feel the oppression of a social system that is inimical to the vast majority of mankind. Capitalism is anti-human, it puts things first and people second. Logically, this system dictates that people too should become things, so that they may better be integrated into a society based on the production and consumption of things. In other words, for the evils that we experience in society today, the capitalist system prescribes anti-consciousness, a suppression of those human characteristics that enable a man to reflect on his environment and judge what is good and bad about it.

To regard this oppressive process as an inevitably determined one is to fall victim to anti-consciousness. The system wants to preserve itself, it is conscious. The system is people, the people that control our environment in all its complex interactions – its legal system, political and cultural institutions, its armed forces, its police, its education, etc. In fact it is those people who we refer to as the ruling class who consciously disseminate anti-consciousness, in an effort to prolong indefinitely their rule, their control.

Unlike these people (who are resisting change), the vast majority of the rest of us feel the 'necessity for change' (39). But if I now go on to say that the change that is necessary is the overthrow of the ruling, controlling class I am probably jumping ahead of a number of people. And in fact I am giving a false impression, an incorrect picture, even though the substance of it is quite right. It is utopian (40): the 'overthrow of the ruling class' is an abstraction, an ideal if I don't regard it from the point of view of the present situation. (In fact in making such a jump I am opening the door to all kinds of ridiculous notions, for example that beings from outer space might overthrow the ruling class, or the working class might suddenly and miraculously wake up to its 'historic mission' to overthrow the ruling class. Such ideas are pure fantasy and cause harm.)

66

In saying that the change that is necessary is the overthrow of the ruling class I am denying or ignoring the fundamental truth that the basis of change is internal, and that external circumstances can only provide favourable or unfavourable conditions for change. The basis for the overthrow of the ruling class lies in the internal weakness of that class. The basis for the victory of the working class lies in the internal strength of the working class. The favourable conditions for the collapse of the ruling class are not only the growing strength and consciousness of the working class, but also the liberation struggles of the colonial and neo-colonial peoples and many other factors. The favourable conditions for the victory of the working class – well, they are so plentiful it is hard to know where to begin. They range from the bankruptcy of imperialist culture and economic problems of imperialism to the shining examples of socialist China and Albania and the worldwide upsurge of revolutionary theory and practice.

It is seen that the victory of one class and the defeat of another form a dialectical unity. It is not their external, superficial strength or weakness that determines the outcome, but their internal, essential structure. The forces of imperialism are outwardly strong, but in the present and forthcoming struggles they will inevitably come to occupy their rightful position in the 'dustbin of history'.

A similarly dialectical process is at work in the development of the revolutionary movement. Here it is the dialectical unity of being and consciousness that is essential. It is fantasy to imagine that the working class and its allies will first became politically conscious and then rise to overthrow the ruling class. The working class and other progressive sections of the population will become politically conscious, fully, only through the actual practice of overthrowing the ruling class in the real world, and then themselves becoming the ruling class.

When, through the social activity and circumstances of our lives we, as individuals, became conscious of the 'necessity for change', we experience the dialectical unity of being and consciousness. At that moment when we genuinely confront the 'necessity for change' in society, a process of change begins *in us*, we begin to grow and develop. We begin to participate in changing society and our consciousness grows alongside this. So, in terms of the individual human being just as in terms of society at large, the basis of change is internal. Outwardly, he tries to create the favourable conditions for this change to go forward. The revolutionary does not do this by retiring to a cave for cultivation of his immortal soul but by ploughing into the struggle against the old and the obsolete, against the decadent and the degenerate, against the human agents of oppression and exploitation (also in the field of culture and art), knowing that practical activity in this struggle provides the best possible external conditions favouring the development not only of his own personal consciousness, but also the consciousness of the vast masses of people who are materially and culturally oppressed under the present social system. In the struggle against the old and decrepit the new is born. In the fight against the political and cultural institutions of imperialism the proletarian revolutionary Party develops the capability to lead the working class in the overthrow of the ruling class.

In the field of music, an ever-increasing number of people are taking the conscious road, in opposition to the anti-conscious (or 'cosmic-conscious') positions adopted by the various 'geniuses' of modern music who tamely – and some say unwittingly – allow their talents to be enlisted on the side of the ruling class. Those composers who take the conscious road necessarily submit to the test of practice. They can no longer take refuge in beautiful ideas, elegance of manner, logical completeness, formal perfection or the 'history of music' (which has no existence separate from social history), and nor do they wish to. In evaluating the work of artists who wish to be conscious, we must place content above form, effect above motive, the essential above the superficial. Rzewski and Wolff are two such artists, who have chosen explicitly political subject matter for their recent works. So the points we should discuss in connection with their works are : what are they saying in their pieces, to whom are they saying it, and whom does it benefit? What effect did they intend to achieve with such works and what effect are they actually achieving? Does the literal, superficial content of their work conceal a deeper, essential content and, if so, what aspects of the real world are reflected in this deeper content?

ACCOMPANIMENTS : TEXT AND PROGRAMME NOTE

The text for *Accompaniments I* is taken from an English translation of *China: the Revolution Continued* by Jan Myrdal and Gun Kessle. The speakers are a veterinarian and a midwife in the village of Liu Ling in the area of Yenan in Northwest China.

Veterinarian (male voice singing): 'My mother is very old now. I asked for leave of absence to go and see her. In such cases we're always granted leave. Obviously.

'There are those who call looking after sick animals dirty work. But Chairman Mao has taught us not to be afraid of filth and excrement. And that's right. Chairman Mao has pointed out how necessary it is to develop stockbreeding. And that's why we are getting ourselves more and more animals and why I'm studying all the time.'

Midwife (female voice singing): 'We've been successful in our work. Now the new-born babies don't die any more. Formerly 60 per cent of all new-born infants died. The old way of giving birth to children was unhygienic. Dangerous both for mother and child. To begin with it was necessary to spread a greal deal of information. But now there are no more problems over childbirth. Now the women understand why hygiene is important. Today, I deliver all the women in the village.

'I'm also responsible for infant care. I teach the women. It's cleanliness that's so important. Their clothes must be clean, their hands must be clean. Their food must be clean. Cleanliness is the answer to disease. It is thanks to cleanliness our babies are surviving. Now the women too understand that three or four years should go by between pregnancies. Pregnancies that are too close together are damaging to health. Formerly many women were always pregnant. Most now understand that this is bad.

'But we must go on spreading information. There used to be some men who spoke against contraception. It was easier to convince the women. But now even none of the men are against them. Now everyone says they agree. But some families are thoughtless. And of course there are accidents too. Today condoms are much cheaper than they were seven years ago. Now they cost only one yuan per hundred. And no one is so poor he can't afford that.

'Other things are more problematic. There are so many bad old customs which must be combatted. There are those who aren't careful enough about their food. Not everyone looks after their latrines properly. Dry earth must be used for covering them. There must be no flies. We have got quite a long way with our hygienic work but not the whole way. That is why unremitting propaganda is needed against the old bad habits. Not to look after latrines properly, that's one such bad habit. Hygiene is a political question. The old bad habits are deep-rooted, but we're fighting them all the time, and things are getting better every year that goes by.

'This work we do during study meetings. To study and apply Mao Tsetung Thought is a good method. Good things can be praised. During these studies many people have come to realise that latrines too are a political question.'

Wolff wrote to me (41) that the piece had been written in response to a request from Rzewski for a piano piece. He had the feeling that texts should be associated with whatever he wrote, if possible. The accompaniment chords had been worked out previously but he had not known what to do with them. For a number of reasons he had been reading about Marxism and about China, where (as he says) it really seems to be happening. The text struck him because it was direct and plain, practical – about important matters (sanitation, contraception) which are ordinary, almost beneath the notice of 'serious', intellectual people; and because these matters are treated in a coherent and positive way, in relation to life as a whole, i.e. politically. He says the text expresses a sense of change in ordinary, specific problems necessarily related to change in the structure of society as a whole. He also chose the text because it was not 'propaganda' in the usual sense, but just statement of fact by the people experiencing it. His motive was to publicise the spirit of the text in a way he thought he could manage and that was congenial, i.e. with that music. He also had the notion that that music had an appropriate feeling (the formal ideas involve movement in cycles that also move forward and, incidentally, gradually upward, by transposition).

This performance is interspersed with instrumental interludes from *Accompaniments IV*. About this music Wolff says it came as a response to the spirit of the text and was written very rapidly, i.e. freely, within a few simple and, he hoped, clarifying restrictions, mostly harmonic, meant to give coherence and, again, a sense of moving forward. He says it is an attempt to write music with elements, melodic and harmonic, that are more directly and generally accessible than his earlier music.

The piece was originally conceived to be played by one person, Rzewski, whose performance as a pianist would be professional and as a singer, amateur. Wolff says that this mixture was deliberate, since the division between professional and amateur is something we've long been trying to break down.

Wolff's score divides the text into groups of 1, 2, 4, 8 or 16 syllables, each group associated with a set of 16 four-note chords. One of these chords, a different one each time, is used to accompany each syllable of the text. Much is left to the performer to decide; the choice and order and timbre of the accompaniment chords, the rhythm and melody of the text (the score says simply that it is to be delivered 'simply'), etc. One could say that Wolff had provided the material but not the composition.

For this performance four composers worked on the material: Howard Skempton composed the rhythm, Chris May composed and instrumented the accompaniment as well as some of the instrumental interludes from *Accompaniments IV*, Janet Danielson wrote the voice parts, and I initiated and coordinated the work of these composers (42).

COMING TOGETHER AND *ATTICA*: TEXT AND PROGRAMME NOTE

Text (spoken without accompaniment): 'In September 1971 inmates of the state prison at Attica in the state of New York, unable to endure further the intolerable conditions existing there, revolted and succeeded in capturing a part of the institution, as well as a number of guards, whom they held as hostages. Foremost among their demands during the ensuing negotiations was the recognition of their right 'to be treated as human beings'. After several days of inconclusive bargaining, Governor Rockefeller ordered state troopers in to retake the prison by force, justifying his action on the grounds that the lives of the hostages were in danger. In the slaughter that followed, forty-three persons lost their lives, including several of the hostages. One of these was Sam Melville, a political prisoner already known for his leadership in the Columbia riots and one of the leaders in the rebellion at Attica. According to some accounts, Sam was only slightly wounded in the assault. The exact cause of his death remains a mystery. The text for the following piece is taken from a letter that Sam wrote from Attica in the spring of 1971.'

(Declaimed with musical backing): 'I think the combination of age and a greater coming together is responsible for the speed of the passing time. It's six months now, and I can tell you truthfully, few periods in my life have passed so quickly. I am in excellent physical and emotional health. There are doubtless subtle surprises ahead, but I feel secure and ready. As lovers will contrast their emotions in times of crisis so am I dealing with my environment. In the indifferent brutality, the incessant noise, the experimental chemistry of food, the ravings of lost hysterical men, I can act with clarity and meaning. I am deliberate, sometimes even calculating, seldom employing histrionics except as a test of the reactions of others. I read much, exercise, talk to guards and inmates, feeling for the inevitable direction of my life.'

(Spoken without accompaniment): 'One of the leaders of the rising in Attica prison was Richard X. Clark. On February 8th 1972, Clark was set free from Attica. As the car that was taking him to Buffalo passed the Attica village limits, he was asked how it felt to put Attica behind him. He said:

(Declaimed with musical backing): 'Attica is in front of me.'

Programme notes (supplied by Rzewski): *Coming Together*, for a speaker and variable instrumental ensemble, was composed in January 1972. The text on which the composition is based, a letter written by Sam Melville in the spring of 1971, describes in eight terse sentences the writer's experience of passing time in prison. In the musical setting, each sentence is broken into seven parts, which are spoken at regular intervals; each sentence is heard seven times. The written music, a single continuous melodic line built of seven pitches, is a precisely defined structure within which a certain amount of improvisation is possible. The title refers both to a passage in the text and to the specific improvisational technique used. *Attica* is a shorter piece based on a quotation of Richard X. Clark with a similar but simpler structure.

Both compositions deal with a historical event : the uprising and massacre at Attica Correctional Facility in September 1971. They do not make a reasoned political statement about the event. They reproduce personal documents relating to it, and attempt to heighten the feelings expressed in them by underscoring them with music. There is therefore a certain ambiguity between the personal, emotional, and meditative aspect of the texts, which is enhanced by cumulative repetition, and their wider political implications. I believe this ambiguity can be either a strength or a weakness in performance, depending on the degree to which the performer identifies personally with the revolutionary struggle taking place in America's prisons and the world at large. (43)

A REPORT ON THE CONCERT

The concert can be reviewed from several points of view. First, from my own point of view, the concert was very useful : I made many mistakes and we can learn from these by negative example. I'll go into the mistakes at the end.

The concert was also useful to me in that it provided a shared experience, a basis for future discussion and activity amongst the çircle of my acquaintance in Berlin, thus breaking out of a situation of isolation and hearsay; my isolation from practising musicians in Berlin, their hearsay about my activities.

This all seems very personal. Nevertheless, in view of the frequent reproaches received about using music as a pretext for politics, etc., it is important to see that all these things are interwoven : people's personal lives, their individual consciousness, their class consciousness, their cultural habits, their political leanings or allegiance.

The second point of view is that of Rzewski and Wolff. A friendly contact exists with these composers and on this basis constructive criticism can be developed.

Coming Together is a piece which deals with a local event, the Attica prison uprising, occurring in a worldwide context of liberation struggles. It is very important material and highly suitable for musical treatment. The error of the piece is that it treats of its subject in a subjective way. The text is fragmented and repeated according to a mechanical plan, with the result that it becomes obsessive. The instrumental accompaniment, which refers to popular music and does actually engage the pop-conscious audience and is a good initiative to that extent, nevertheless develops a negative aspect of pop music – its hypnotic or hysterical aspect – and none of its positive aspects.

The basic ideology of the piece is anarchism. I say. this not because Sam Melville was an anarchist (I don't know if he was or not), but on account of the choice and treatment of this text for this purpose. The political activities springing from anarchism are reformism and terrorism, which is something we ·did not bring out clearly enough in the discussion. We came up against an important political theme and did not discuss it properly. The dialectical unity of reformism and terrorism was not brought out for example. For instance : in Northern Ireland the Civil Rights Movement ('a fair deal for Catholics') and the IRA are two sides of the same coin : they are both pleading for the most flagrant injustices to be removed, so that class relations can continue as before (44).

Anarchism is an ideology that springs from the decaying bourgeoisie. From the wreckage of broken bourgeois promises (e.g., individual freedom, etc.) the anarchist wants to leap into absolutes : 'total freedom', 'no government at all', etc. Its bourgeois origin is evident from the fact that it plays down the class struggle and the role of the masses in making history.

Hence, although this piece could potentially find some acceptance amongst the youth, as far as its language is concerned, it would not find acceptance amongst the class-conscious proletariat, since its ideology is not proletarian and in fact is not far removed from Mick Jagger's 'I can't get no satisfaction', and contributes just as little to revolutionary change. Marxists should therefore militate against the introduction of such works amongst the masses – they get too much of this already.

Accompaniments, in the version we prepared, met with a totally blank reception from the audience, and I gather that things were not much warmer when the piece was first played by Rzewski in the USA. Why don't people respond to the piece? I think Wolff's mistake is in thinking that if something is simple it can be easily understood. This leads to the corrupt equation: simple = popular, implying that the masses are simple-minded. In fact in a complex world simplicity is achieved only by a process of abstraction, and abstractions are not easily grasped. Especially not by the masses whose daily activity tends to be more practical and hence has to deal constantly with the complexity of the real world. At some points in our version there were hints of that kind of simplicity that characterises a fairy story or a lullaby, but they were only hints and the context was lacking in which they could have been effective (45).

The main criticism of Wolff's piece centred on why this text was selected. The intuitive scepticism that had greeted this piece when I tried to introduce it to the Scratch Orchestra last year was illuminated by a flash of lightning when I received Christian's notes on the piece, in which he mentions the themes of the text as 'sanitation and birth-control'. Of course: pollution and the population explosion, two of the great red herrings (secondary contradictions) that the bourgeoisie has brought out in the last few years in an attempt to distract people's attention from the principal contradiction, capital and labour. I don't imagine that Christian scoured the annals of the Chinese Revolution with specific intention of finding material that would be of use for a bourgeois propaganda campaign. But it's important to remember that there are whole armies of academics and journalists doing just that, and the fact that Christian was innocently drawn into something similar (though on a small scale) says something about how intensively and unremittingly we've got to fight against bourgeois ideology if we're ever going to manage more than 'one step forward, two steps back'.

From the point of view of the audience the concert was confusing. In the old Scratch Orchestra we used to work hard to create confusion, such confusion that the mind could no longer grapple with the overall situation and would thus submit voluntarily to the enslavement of 'mere phenomena'. In this concert there were extenuating circumstances and positive aspects to the confusion, but avantgardists have to be on their guard against such notions that confusion is a good thing 'in itself' because it dialectically gives rise to clarity, and similar intellectual artifices.

Some false preconceptions were attacked. For instance, the idea that the musician or conductor (or even the composer) identifies with the music he presents. It became apparent that we had presented this music in order to criticise it. This seemed to create a slight sense of shock. But obviously it's essential that an intellectual audience takes a critical attitude to art, and this means, in the present wave of superficially political art works (such as Warhol's Mao prints, to take a crass example), developing the political criteria to deal with them. Often artists do not consciously support the political line that their art reflects, so when an artist reflects a bourgeois political line in his work (as do Rzewski and Wolff) this does not mean that we should necessarily regard him as a scheming enemy; there is a good chance that he is actually an erring brother. The path that should be pointed out to such artists is the path of investigation and study. Along this path it quickly becomes clear that there is no such thing as investigation and study above classes and then the most crucial matter comes into the foreground : integrating with the masses. This is summed up in the slogan : 'Seek truth from facts to serve the people.'

One interesting fact about the composition of the audience for avantgarde music came out. Besides the regular fans and cliques there are quite a few people who come on spec hoping to hear something new and above all something that means something. They are invariably disappointed and never reappear, but there are always more where they came from. Hence the fact that though the avantgarde audience does not grow, it does not disappear entirely.

Now for the mistakes. In planning and organising the concert I gave the music a secondary role and the discussion the primary role. So far, so good. What I failed to take into account was that the primary role cannot be played properly if the secondary role is not played properly. The choice of instrumentalists, the preparation of parts, the amount of rehearsal time necessary – all these things I treated in a summary way, leaving it in the hands of others, while concentrating myself on the discussion material. The result was that we almost didn't have anything to discuss. Also, although there was some discussion and struggle amongst the musicians during rehearsal, it failed to develop strongly simply because of the pressure of work.

We learn from this that if you present something for criticism you must present it legibly. It was not a question of criticising Rzewski and Wolff personally (as if to say, you've gone wrong and deserve everything you get in the way of bad performances, etc.), but criticising their ideological and political lines, which also exist in the audience's minds and in our own. Our aim should have been, with the aid of this music, to bring these ideological and political lines out into the open and take a conscious stand against them and criticise them. By not presenting the music strongly enough we failed to generate that sense of community (basis of all music-making) in which a meaningful discussion could have taken place – i.e. a discussion leading to a degree of unity at least among a section of those present.

20.5.73

CHAPTER 4

Self-Criticism: Repudiation of Earlier Works

Someone taking a stand, digging his heels in, making judgements on the basis of political criteria not only provokes a response (positive, in that the ideas put forward are taken up in discussion) but also a reaction (negative, in that people are knocked off balance and retaliate in a wild and flailing manner). The reaction to the criticism of Cage and Stockhausen often took the form. 'What about your music? Your music is just as bourgeois and backward as theirs'. Maybe such critics hoped I would feel obliged to defend my own music and thus inevitably return to the straight and narrow path of servile ideologist of the bourgeoisie. Treacherous solicitude! The fact is that everything is involved in the process of change, including my ideas, and I make no bones about having produced music just as backward as anything a Cage or a Stockhausen is capable of. The main thing is not the mistakes one makes, but one's ability to learn from them and change direction.

The bourgeoisie has now given me two opportunities publicly to repudiate my own earlier compositions.

The first opportunity presented itself as an invitation to contribute to an 'International Symposium on the Problematic of Today's Musical Notation' held in Rome from 23–26 October 1972. About 100 scientists, musicologists, educationalists and composers were invited (no fee, but all expenses paid, even from the remotest corners of the globe) to contribute to this 'symposium' on a non-existernt problem (46). I participated in the symposium quite militantly, taking sides on a number of issues and refusing to vanish into thin air at the crack of any absurdly abstruse scientific or philosophical whip. The venue was the monumental neo-fascist edifice of the Institute Latino-

Americano. The furnishings were plush in the extreme: individual arm-chairs fitted with head-phones providing simultaneous translation into four languages. My own contribution took the form of a talk on my composition Treatise, *a 200-page so-called 'graphic score' composed 1963–67 as an attempt to escape from the performance rigidities of serial music and encourage improvisation amongst avantgarde musicians.*

TALK FOR ROME SYMPOSIUM ON PROBLEMS OF NOTATION

What are the problems of musical notation today? There is no problem in dealing with new sounds on instruments, since the number of new symbols that can be devised is unlimited. On the other hand there are musical problems created by the systematic exploitation of the complexities available in the notation, for example in the avantgarde music of the 1950s – but that would be the subject of a different symposium. In that music it's often not the music that's serial but the scores (47).

One might imagine problems of notation arising where the inspiration of the music is divorced from the fundamental assumptions of western musical notation, for instance if you want to write music that doesn't progress through rhythmic units, or that doesn't restrict itself to the division of the octave into twelve equal parts, or if your method of composing is by manipulating tape and you need a score not for production purposes but as a means to study formal relationships already existing in sound (on tape). However, it is probable that the inspiration of modern composers cannot escape the influence of the conventions of our music notation, and problems of this sort are likely to be soluble by extensions of the existing framework of notation conventions.

What I want to talk about is not such problems as these but what I feel to be diseases of notation, cases where the notation seems to have become a malignant growth usurping an absolutely unjustifiable pre-eminence over the music. I feel obliged to study these diseases on my own body, in my own work, rather than as they are evident elsewhere in the avantgarde. One reason for this is that I can diagnose them with far greater certainty in the context of my own development than in someone else's and also I can speak with greater authority and full consciousness about the harmful effect of these diseases and how they hamper rather than enhance any development in one's musical thinking.

So far I have identified two main diseases : first, the idea that each composition requires or deserves its own unique system of notation. Let's be more accurate : the composer doesn't conceive of a piece of music so much as a notation system, which musicians may then use as a basis for making music, or more likely (as I would evaluate it today), aimless manipulations of the system in terms of sound (48).

Second, the idea that a musical score can have some kind of aesthetic identity of its own, quite apart from its realisation in sound, in other words that the score is a visual art work, the appreciation of which *may* depend on a consciousness of music and sound and the ways they have been notated, but with no certainty that the ideas of the composition can be transferred into and expressed through the world of sound. In my output I was preoccupied for several years with a large-scale manifestation of this second disease, the graphic score *Treatise*, and it is to this work that I wish to apply some more detailed criticism.

Of course diseases of this kind do not arise spontaneously. We must get to their roots and understand how they grow and what plants them and nourishes them. Then, as in medicine, the correct method is to devise a strategy for eliminating the root causes of a disease and tactics for dealing with its symptoms until such time as they disappear.

An adequately planned criticism of a work of avantgarde art might proceed as follows :

First, to look at the score itself, to go into the superficial formal contradictions manifested, in the case of *Treatise*, in the graphic work.

Second, to try and uncover the ideas that it embodies, expose its content, and see whether these ideas are right or wrong, whether they truly reflect what we know about the real world.

Third, to examine the cultural environment of the avantgarde, the place of the avantgarde within the general production of music today.

Fourth, to see the social and economic factors that produce and mould that cultural environment.

These social and economic factors are not standing still, they are changing and developing. A result of this is the conflict between progressive forces, which recognise the inevitability or the necessity for change and actively promote it, and reactionary forces, which oppose change. This conflict is fought out in the realm of politics. The decisive thing is : who holds political power? and here I don't mean which political party but which *class* holds political power? At this point we should move on with our critical programme :

Fifth, to see how political power – and in capitalist society this means virtually 'money' – controls the manifestations of the fundamental conflict in the cultural environment, including the avantgarde.

Sixth, to recognise the ideas, the world outlook, represented by a particular piece of avantgarde music as being the ideas characteristic of the ruling class, ideas that do not challenge that class and its power, and hence support its continued existence.

Seventh, because these ideas are reactionary and do not accurately reflect the present stage of our knowledge of the world we see that their forms of expression (say, the graphic work of *Treatise*) are contradictory and incoherent, like the words of a liar who has lost all hope of deceiving his audience.

So it becomes clear that the roots of those diseases lie in society, not in the minds of misguided composers. Society develops through class antagonisms; bourgeois society is produced by the domination of the capitalist class and the subjugation of the working class. Bourgeois society was once immensely progressive in many fields, especially in the field of industrial production and also in the field of culture and artistic production. But bourgeois society is now in the last stages of decay and is the victim of countless diseases, including inflation, the pollution of the atmosphere, and cultural degeneracy. Does the fact that the roots of all our cultural ills lie in society absolve the individual artist from all responsibility for these ills? Certainly not. As Marx said of philosophy, 'It is not enough to understand the world, the point is to change it', so we should say to artists, 'It is not enough to decorate the world, the point is to influence it.'

The strategy for eliminating the root causes of our present artistic diseases is the same strategy as is needed for eliminating the root causes of most of the evils of society today, namely the overthrow of monopoly capitalism and the bourgeois state and its replacement by socialism.

The great thing for artists to realise is that this step involves all sections of society including themselves. Having seen that the cultural environment is moulded by who holds political power, the artist must then quite consciously take a political stand in his art and life, and it certainly does not contradict the instincts of the bourgeois artist of the 'good old days' to take a progressive stand and not a reactionary one (49); the one thing that has to change is his class allegiance. The bourgeois artist was never essentially a capitalist, he worked in the service of capitalism in its progressive stage. Now he should work in the service of the progressive, revolutionary class of the present, the working class. In doing so he is no longer a bourgeois artist coping with incurable cultural diseases but a proletarian artist participating in the fight to change the world.

Such a change is not the work of a moment. For the composer it is not only a question of making a decision but of changing one's ideas. It is in this area that some tactics for coping with the symptoms of our cultural diseases are useful. The main tactic that I have in mind is criticism, and that's why I outlined that 7-point critical method.

Such a critical method should be used on works that have a large effect on a large audience, in order to expose their true character and minimise their harmful effect. Happily for my peace of mind *Treatise* has not been so successful, and I am treating it merely as a test case. Rather than waste time on a systematic study of something which, though large, is of small importance, I want just to talk about some of the salient features.

In criticising art we should proceed from the basic standpoint that art contains ideas; it is an expression of consciousness, not just a phenomenon of the natural world, or a documentation of such a phenomenon. We live in the world, and our ideas are about the world. The sum total of our ideas constitutes our world outlook. Ideas are right or wrong in proportion as they reflect truly or distort the world (50). They are relevant or irrelevant in proportion as they reflect the forces that are most active in the world today. The most active forces in the world today are not cosmic forces, or atomic forces, or spiritual forces (whatever they may be), but the social forces, the forces generated by large groupings of human beings.

Let's start with the idea – very widespread in the avantgarde and implicit in the score of *Treatise* – that anything can be transformed into anything else. Now everybody knows (not only Marxists and farmers) that a stone, no matter how much heat you apply to it, will never hatch into a chicken. And that even an egg won't hatch into a chicken without the right external conditions. And yet in Cage's work *Atlas Eclipticalis* patterns of stars in a star atlas are transformed into a jumble of electronic squeals and groans. This transformation is carried out through a system of notation (a logic) that has no connection with astronomy and only a very sketchy connection with music.

In *Gruppen* Stockhausen transforms formant analyses of vocal sounds into flurries of notes on orchestral instruments. In *Structures* Boulez transforms numerical systems into random successions of sound on two pianos. In graphic music a string of visual symbols is transformed into sound. True, there is a distinction between the Cage example and the other examples. Cage consciously refrains from imposing an image on the material generated by his transformations, whereas Stockhausen and Boulez do just that – they convert their fragmented material into a semblance of musical form, just as a mass of string can be shaped into the semblance of a human being; these semblances should of course be studied and criticised, from the point of view that the images of art should intensify, not falsify, our consciousness of the world.

Nevertheless, this distinction between Cage and the others is more apparent than real. Though Cage may refrain from forming his material into images, society does it for him – his works are played in concerts and hence are listened to as pieces of music, and the audience does its best to relate them to the world of their experience. And actually that's not too hard, for in its effect Cage's music does give an approximate reflection of some aspects of present-day life under capitalism. *Concert for Piano* sounds like a chaotic welter of individualistic conflicts, without harmony, without purpose. *HPSCHD* creates an image of society as a jumble of sense stimuli, flashing lights and tinkling sounds, in which the individual is reduced to the position of a mere spectator. These negative, pessimistic effects created by Cage's music reflect the surface character of the capitalist world, they do not reflect its essence. They don't indicate the direction of its change and development and worst of all they deny the positive contribution that individuals are capable of making towards this change.

Change is absolute, there is nothing that does not change. But it is just a stupid pun to say, on this basis, that everything is interchangeable, or by your actions to imply any such belief. Summer changes to winter, iron ore is changed into steel, a sequence of notes can be changed into a melody, but a tree can never be changed into a saucer of milk. Not in the real world. But in avantgarde art it can (the artist might saw down the tree, scoop out a hollow and fill it with milk), and this is not only irrelevant to the social struggles going on in the world, but on a very fundamental level it is distorting reality, propagating lies, wrong ideas, about the real world. George Brecht's (51) work on paradoxes is on this level – it operates on the pretence that a paradox can have a concrete existence and is more than just an error of formulation. Such artists of course defend themselves with humour. But society needs art, it needs artists, quite seriously, that's why it has always produced them and it is not going to be satisfied with a bunch of intellectuals cracking jokes amongst themselves.

There are right ideas and wrong ones about the history of music. It is correct to say that music is produced to fulfil the needs of a society and that vast amounts, in particular, are produced to fulfil the need of the ruling class in that society to hold the subject classes down ideologically. It is quite incorrect to say that music is a world of its own, developing according to its own internal laws. It is, if possible, even more incorrect to say that musical *notation* is a world of its own, developing according to its own internal laws. And yet this seems to be the premise on which *Treatise* is composed. As it says in the *Treatise Handbook* (a collection including the notes I made while working on *Treatise*), 'The way the elements act on each other – it is like chemical processes: acid bites, circles roll and drag, and bend the stave lines of "musical space" '. *Treatise* arbitrarily combines images of transformations that occur in the real world : images of mathematical or logical transformations (multiplication of elements, relations between pairs of dissimilar elements, presence and absence of elements), and of physical transformations (by fragmentation, exploding, squashing, bending, melting, interpenetrating, etc.). And in amongst all these visual abstractions from reality a host of devices are used to keep the reader amused : 3-dimensional effects, pictorial effects, hints at concrete objects (trees, clouds, etc.) and enigmatic musical symbols.

This fits very well with what I said about the incoherence of the liar who has lost all hope of deceiving his listeners. He is quite likely to turn then to diversionary tactics, just as a child does in a situation of embarrassment : standing on his head, singing a silly song, knocking over a jug of milk or simply pretending to be mad. Anyway, in *Treatise* the effect of these devices is as minimal as that of the *Notenbild*, the visual aspect of a traditional score – an undefined, subjective stimulus for the interpreter.

In performance, the score of *Treatise* is in fact an obstacle between the musicians and the audience.

Behind that obstacle the musicians improvise, but instead of improvising on the basis of objective reality and communicating something of this to the audience, they preoccupy themselves with that contradictory artefact : the score of *Treatise*. So not only is *Treatise* an embodiment of (not only irrelevant but also) incorrect ideas, it also effectively prevents the establishment of communication between the musicians and the audience.

Musical graphics are a substitute for composition. It is a truly laughable situation when you can compose a piece of 'music' without ever having heard or played a note of music. In fact nowadays you don't even have to use pen and ink, you can get a computer to draw it for you.

It is interesting to see from my own experience how the avant-garde fights tooth and nail in support of its incorrect ideas. In the early days of writing *Treatise* (1963) I was studying the work of Frege (52). In the *Handbook* I quote two phrases of his : 'The mysterious power of words devoid of thought', and 'No one will expect any sense to emerge from empty symbols'. Quite right. Words devoid of thought have the power only to mystify and confuse, and no sense will ever emerge from empty symbols. And yet, despite Rzewski's very reasonable suggestion that I should abandon the piece, I persevered with it for four more years.

What more graphic illustration of the astounding tenacity of bourgeois ideology, and what more telling indication of how ruthlessly that ideology must now be fought against in the avant-garde !

How to account for this 'astounding tenacity' of bourgeois ideology in the avantgarde? To quote the *Handbook* again : 'Psychologically, the existence of *Treatise* is fully explained by the situation of the composer who is not in a position to make music' (53). The avantgarde is isolated. By the process of alienation which has been going forward in giant strides since the beginning of the century, the modern composer has become isolated both from the working musicians and from any audience except a tiny intellectual elite. So, although the state will continue to support it and even promote some kind of audience for it, such support and such audience cannot cover up the fact that the avantgarde is in desperate straits. It represents bourgeois ideology with its back to the wall.

The ideology of a ruling class is present in its art implicitly; the ideology of a revolutionary class must be expressed in its art explicitly. Progressive ideas must shine like a bright light into the dusty cobwebs of bourgeois ideology in the avantgarde, so that any genuinely progressive spirits working in the avantgarde find their way out, take a stand on the side of the people and set about making a positive contribution to the revolutionary movement.

During the symposium I made a number of shorter contributions and I publish these notes here for the sake of local colour, to give an impression of what the symposium was actually like.

ADDITIONAL MATERIAL PRESENTED IN THE COURSE OF DISCUSSION

There is a great difference between the remarks in my talk about notation problems and the statements of the scientists. I say that all problems of notation will be solved by the masses, i.e.

through the efforts of working musicians and composers and also teachers and musicologists, engaged in the practical activities of music. What makes the scientists' position so difficult is that they want to study and analyse a language (or create a meta-language) in the laboratory, without contact with the people who speak it, and without interest in what is being said (they are only interested in *how* it says things). In this they reflect an attitude that is rife amongst composers – the tendency to become preoccupied with form to the exclusion of content.

The case of the Hukwe song in Carpitezza's (54) lecture was revealing. Of course the early transcribers of ethnic music were quite naive in their 'eurocentrism'. But what the talk brought out was that no progress has been made, only more sophistication. Music cannot be understood except in its social context. In any case let's think what the motive force is in ethnomusicology and related studies. Civilisation is destroying primitive man. The idea is to *take possession* of his resources. (Brazil, where they go out hunting Indians.) In order to convert the resources of primitive man – primarily his land – into bourgeois property, imperialism exterminates the people and, as a preliminary to this, it has his culture transcribed and makes this into bourgeois property too.

It is interesting that the same property relations can be seen in the field of pop music today. Many records are made without benefit of anything written. However, all pop records are transcribed, something is written down, because this is the only way the musicians can establish copyright, can assert their private ownership of the music.

In tackling the question of musical *content*, Stefani (55) takes up a number of avenues and subdivides many of them. So we find under section 4 the two subdivisions denotative and connotative meaning, and in the last of eight subdivisions of the field of connotative meaning, we find what he calls 'global axiological connotations'. He says, 'as any other reality, the musical work can form the object of moral and political evaluations'.

Most composers would agree that a composition is not an 'object to be evaluated' (property again), but a force to influence the consciousness of living people and *as such* it functions morally and politically. So this point should not be at the end of some remote cul-de-sac of the musicologists' categorisation, but in the direct forefront, occupying most of the screen. To what is the rest of his paper devoted? I don't pretend to understand it all, but it is obvious that if the most relevant aspect is dealt with in two lines and the paper is 24 pages long, there is a great deal that is irrelevant.

Of course there is a reply to this. I came up against it in connection with Ashley's (56) talk – someone said, 'that's all very fine but this is a conference about notation, and Ashley just changed the subject and referred to politics.' There are two points to be made here. Firstly, it is good to change the subject from something unimportant to something important. And in dealing with unimportant things (as we all have to do in daily life) it is *vital* to see them *in relation* to the important things. And in this sense, Ashley's talk was a positive contribution.

Secondly, it is the conscious tactics of a ruling class in a weak position to bring up unimportant points and treat them as important. This conference is an example – problems of notation are secondary to musical problems, musical problems are secondary to social and political problems. As one of the organisers pointed out, it has been quite easy to organise this very expensive conference devoted to a very minor issue, but if you want to get money from the state to improve music education in schools you come up against complete refusal.

So in the question of what is relevant we have to use our own minds, and not assume that something is relevant just because a lot of fuss is being made about it, conferences convened, etc.

It isn't possible to see the Brown/Evangelisti controversy as an isolated instance (57). This is rampant in the avantgarde. People like Kurt Stone (58) would like to do something to improve it. But with little chance of success, because these are symptoms of a very deep decay in avantgarde music. Bad performances are so commonplace it is impossible for the composer any longer to imagine that this situation somehow has nothing to do with him, that he is innocent. In fact it wasn't just Earle's piece, the whole concert was bad and boring, the notations have failed to engage the energies of the performers. Even conventionally notated pieces fail to do this; performances are lifeless. So this problem is not specific to graphic music.

What a storm in a teacup. Individuals attack each other and there is great disunity. What is needed is for each person to take a sober look at his own activity in the context of the world political situation, and also in the context of his local involvement in a musical community, and come to a point of readiness to work together to produce a positive atmosphere and real development.

Our main subject should be : what progressive role can avantgarde composers and musicologists play in society? Widmer (59) and Stone are two examples whose work is socially directed, for the use of teachers, children, students, musicians. They put collective needs above their individual inclinations (up to a point). Nattiez (60) is the opposite – he is fascinated by the possibility that music and language (and possibly also microbiological sequences) have formal features in common. He experiences a kind of scientific ecstasy in thinking about this and wants everyone to share his enthusiasm. Many composers also seem to feel this way about their work.

I have characterised these two lines – following one's own inclination and fulfilling the needs of society – in different people, who we might say are mainly one or the other. However each single person has these two lines in himself, sometimes they may even completely coincide (for example if a man is following his own inclination in serving the needs of society) and sometimes be completely divorced (follow your inclination at the weekend, and serve society during the week) (61).

Now if everyone in the avantgarde could bring these two forces into equilibrium – their self-centred delight in their own activity and the consciousness of being active on behalf of the community – such enormous energy would be released that the problems of the avantgarde would disappear overnight.

The forces fighting against this are : the philosophy of individualism (which is being promoted in all education) and the bourgeois state, the protector of the capitalists whose interests are in direct conflict with the interests of the masses of the people.

Of course I am not interested in solving the problems of the bourgeoisie (if I could provide a contented avantgarde to replace the discontented one, I'd probably be in clover for the rest of my life). This is why we have to study politics and ideology. We must learn that if we become good children and serve our governments faithfully, we are definitely acting *against* the interest of the vast majority of the people. In balancing the individual and the collective we must become conscious of *which* collective, *which* class, it is whose interests we should put above our own. We must take our stand on the side of the working and oppressed people, the class that is in direct opposition to the ruling class and the state machinery under its control.

So it is definitely *possible* for composers and musicologists of the avantgarde to take a progressive role. It is possible through resolving the contradiction between the individual and the collective approach and by developing class consciousness. The next question is : what role ? It is too soon to answer this, but for a start we should take a general look at the vast field of musical production and realise that the avantgarde is just a tiny pocket in that. An objective view of music consumption shows this. So it must be seminal – this is the only way we can influence things (62). We must put our ideas and our music in such a way that they spread and grow elsewhere in the vast arena of musical production. And with this in mind we should take a very solemn and searching look at our music and our ideas and test them by every means available as to whether they are in fact healthy or poisonous, progressive or reactionary.

At this conference there has been a struggle :
– on one side, the musicians, who wish to throw out the original subject of the symposium because notation is unimportant relative to music, which again is less important than the social situation in which it occurs.
– on the other side the musicologists, who constantly wish to return to the problem of notation because it is the lifeline of their work.
This struggle is divergent – it cannot be resolved in the symposium. The scientists with whom the musicians might have liked to work are the scientists occupied with studying perception, the brain and the nervous system, or the physical properties of sound, acoustics. Obviously such scientists could not be called to a symposium on notation. So we see that the decisive factor was

the original selection of the subject for the symposium – this determined the selection of speakers, which made it impossible for the conference to lead to progress in the field of musical production.

Treatise was a large-scale opus on which I wasted more hours of craftsmanship and intellectual effort than I care to recall. It would gratify me to sell the manuscript to a sleepy bourgeois at an inflated price and thus receive at least some compensation for that waste.

The Great Learning (1968–71) was an even larger-scale opus and, because it definitely promotes a reactionary ideological content (Confucianism) and because some of its techniques of performance are effective and could potentially carry it beyond the confines of the avantgarde, it merits criticism from a wider viewpoint than that of the avantgarde. The opportunity to criticise it came up on the occasion of a performance of the first two paragraphs at the Berlin Philharmonic Hall in March 1974. I decided to accept the engagement with the proviso that I would write a relatively comprehensive article describing the nature of the piece and what I thought about it, and distribute this article to the concert audience and attempt to have the article used on all subsequent occasions when the piece might be brought before the public, e.g. in broadcasts, etc. In this way the reactionary composition can be used not only as an arena for ideological struggle but also as a carrier pigeon for revolutionary ideas. At that time there was a fierce struggle going on in China against Lin Piao's line and the ideas of Confucius and I tried to include my article in that frame of reference.

CRITICISM OF *THE GREAT LEARNING*

This article deals with paragraphs 1 and 2 of *The Great Learning*, my musical rendering of part of one of the Confucian scriptures, equivalent possibly to the Christian credo.

As is the case with all works of art, ideas are being communicated in this music, ideas are being promoted in a particular present-day context, with a particular class character.

Confucian doctrine does not consist of absolute truths any more than does the Christian doctrine. Since class struggle began, well before Confucius's time, ideas have been born in class struggle, are used in class struggle and are constantly re-interpreted and changed in the course of class struggle. This year (1974) Confucius's ideas are at the centre of a veritable storm of struggle in their country of origin, the People's Republic of China. It is in the context of this struggle that I want to evaluate this aspect, the Confucian aspect, of my work *The Great Learning* and form a judgement on it.

The backbone of the ideological content of the work is the Confucian text. This will be dealt with first. But a body does not consist only of backbone; the flesh and blood of *The Great Learning* is sounding musical forms. Though these forms com-municate non-verbally, they also communicate ideas. These forms are the product of historical development and are created for performers to play and for audiences to listen to. They are couched in contemporary musical language and embody ideas reflecting present-day reality, reflecting aspects of the class struggle as it is being waged in our own time. This flesh and blood aspect of the work's ideological content will be dealt with later in the article (63).

Finally I will attempt to evaluate the work from the class standpoint of the working class. From this standpoint the work stands out clearly as a piece of 'inflated rubbish' whose only value is its counter-revolutionary value to the ruling class. This being the case, the question arises : if I am genuinely adopting this standpoint, why do I allow the work to continue in use?

The aim is to use the work (such parts of it as are artistically more or less successful, that have a certain communicative power) as a carrier for its criticism. In this way, wherever the work is played its class character and its ideological content will be brought to light and criticised, and the consciousness of the progressive section of audiences will be raised by repudiating the content of the work itself.

The Place of Confucius in the History of China

The transition from the slave-owning societies of the Yin Dynasty (1520–1030 BC) and the early Chou Dynasty (1030–770 BC) to the feudal society of the Chin Dynasty (221–207 BC) and the Han Dynasty (202 BC–AD 220) was extremely turbulent. There were slave uprisings in the Spring and Autumn Period (770–476 BC), and the Warring States Period (476–221 BC) was characterised by intense political and military struggles. Reflecting these struggles, there was also warfare in the realm of ideas (64). Confucius lived 551–479 BC, at the end of the Spring and Autumn Period, and the Confucian doctrine was developed in the succeeding centuries by generations of disciples, chief among them being Mencius (390–305 BC). *The Great Learning* is thought to have been written by a pupil of Mencius about 260 BC, the first chapter (on which my work is based) being attributed to Confucius himself.

In the ideological struggles of the Warring States Period the Confucians were on the side of reaction. By advocating revival of the old ritual culture they were advocating a return to the old social system of slavery – all under the slogan of 'benevolence and righteousness'. On the other side were the Legalists, a school of political thought that was looking forward to the feudal system which was to unite China under the Chin and Han Dynasties. Shang Yang (d. 338 BC) and Han Fei (280–233 BC) were the chief exponents of legalism. They advocated a well-defined code of law with a system of rewards and punishments to which all classes without exception were to be subject. Their legal system was devised to promote agricultural production and military strength. Many western historians of Chinese thought look askance at the legalists, accusing them of bureaucracy, ruthlessness and other 'crimes'. The fact remains that, after centuries of internal strife, when the Prince of Chin put legalist proposals into practice he was able to unify China in less than ten years, for these proposals conformed to the actual stage of development of Chinese society. The Chin Dynasty was short-lived, but it finally established the feudal system. Later, during the Han Dynasty, the doctrines of Confucius were re-introduced to consolidate the autocratic rule of the feudal lords and lend it a more humanitarian and 'benevolent' appearance. Confucianism became the dominant, official religion in China, and remained so until the overthrow of the Ching (Manchu) Dynasty in 1911.

Backward people defend Confucius against the criticism of the masses in the period of the democratic and socialist revolutions in China

From 1911 to the present the struggle against Confucian ideas has been an integral part of the struggle for national liberation and the socialist construction of New China. The May 4th Movement of 1919 (65) propagated the slogan : 'Down with the old (Confucian) morality; up with the new (democratic) morality'. The present movement to criticise Confucius and Lin Piao homes in on 'restraining oneself and restoring the rites', the Confucian quote with which Lin Piao wanted actually to restrain the forces of socialism and restore capitalism.

Just as in his own day Confucius tried to prop up a decadent and dying social system, so it is the decadent and dying in our own time who try to prop up Confucius. According to Chiang Kai-shek – the stooge of US imperialism who still bleats about his Chinese 'nationalist revolution' from his island exile of Taiwan – Confucius was the 'eternal paragon of correct human relations' and, seeing that the 'traditional doctrine handed down by the sages' is in danger of extinction, he moans that 'this is the biggest misfortune of our country and the biggest sorrow of the nation, and no peril can be greater or more imminent than this' (66). With the downfall of Confucius he sees his own final defeat approaching.

According to Liu Shao-chi, the capitalist-roader who was removed from office during the Great Proletarian Cultural Revolution, the doctrines of Confucius and Mencius were a 'bequest useful to us'. Yes, if it were the desire of the Chinese people to restore capitalism. But this isn't the case and so they have no desire to inherit Confucius.

Lin Piao claimed to have detected historical materialism in the doctrines of Confucius and this attempt to dress up Con-

94

fucius in Marxist clothes is also being undertaken in the Soviet Union. They too claim that 'progressive aspects may be found in the early Confucianists', but one is hardly surprised to find that these progressive aspects are things like 'humanitarianism' and 'love of mankind', familiar enough concepts in the Soviet Union today, where every attempt is made to gloss over the class struggle and propagate an ideal 'State of the Whole People'. (Just as in the West, it is not the exploited and oppressed people in the Soviet Union who gloss over the class struggle, but the ruling class, the new bourgeoisie.) Indeed all these reactionaries seem to have one thing in common: they want to recreate Confucius in their own sugared pill image.

Who promotes Confucius in the West and what for?

In the West he has provided similar opportunities. The early missionary scholars sought Christian ethics in Confucius and found them. Ezra Pound sought the 'philosopher of fascism' and found that in Confucius. Since Pound has been the most active promoter of Confucius outside academic circles in the English-speaking West, and since it was his version of the *Great Learning* that inspired my composition, I will go into his views more thoroughly.

Ezra Pound was an American poet who was active in the literary avantgarde in the '20s, helping to build the reputations of such figures as T. S. Eliot and James Joyce. In the '30s he was an active supporter of fascism. He supported Oswald Mosley in England and publicly supported Mussolini before and during the Second World War, broadcasting his fascist views in English from Rome Radio. He was rabidly anti-semitic and anti-communist and, in a period when monopoly-capitalism and imperialism were on the rampage, he chose to attribute all the evils of the world to 'usury'. Shattered by the outcome of the war he drifted more and more into visions of 'eternal light'.

In 1937, in a magazine *The Aryan Path*, Pound published an article called *The Immediate Need for Confucius* (67). In it he takes up a posture of abject humility before the ancient scripture: 'In considering a value already age-old and never to

95

end while men are, I prefer not to write "to the Modern World". The *Ta Hio (Great Learning)* stands, and the commentator were better advised to sweep a few leaves from the temple steps'. All this reverence is sham; he knows very well what forces in the modern world need Confucius and what for: 'There is a visible and raging need of the *Ta Hio* in barbarous countries like Spain and Russia', obviously for quelling the proletariat! '. . . There is also a question of milder and more continuous hygiene', i.e. to prevent risings of the 'stupid mob' in countries where the proletarian revolution was not currently on the move. Pound would dearly have liked to see the *Great Learning* put into direct political practice in the service of fascism – a wild dream, since the social system for which the *Great Learning* was conceived was already obsolete when the text was written. The political principles of the *Great Learning* never were put into practice and never will be; they function better in the ideological sphere as a means of deception. Pound's plans for it in this direction look like this: 'The whole of Western Idealism is a jungle. Christian theology is a jungle. To think it through, to reduce it to some semblance of order, there is no better axe than the *Ta Hio*.' Again: 'The life of occidental mind fell apart [with the decline of religion] into progressively stupider and still more stupid segregations. Hence the need for Confucius, and specifically of the *Ta Hio*, and more specifically of the first chapter of the *Ta Hio*, which you may treat as a mantram, or as a mantram reinforced, a mantram elaborated so that the meditation may gradually be concentrated into contemplation.'

Pound's aim has been summed up by J. S. Thompson: 'To abstract, from the histories of tyranny and oppression, those things that worked to ensure order, "a world order", the "social co-ordinate of Confucius and Mussolini".' (68)

How the musical Great Learning came into existence

Like many other mis-educated products of a bourgeois up-bringing, it was to the very wildness and contradictoriness of Pound's work that I fell victim when in 1968, stimulated by a commission from McNaghten Concerts for the Cheltenham Festival, I decided to make a musical version of the first chapter of his *Great Learning* translation. As a politically backward composer wrapped up in the abstractions of the avantgarde, I was not concerned about Pound's politics and it mattered little to me that his mystical interpretation contradicted the findings of most scholars. I had not read and would not have heeded Shang Yang's warning about ancient texts: 'Anyone who studies ancient texts without a teacher, trying to discover what they mean merely by the use of his own intelligence, will not to his dying day make out either the words or their general meaning.' Pound of course set great store by his own intelligence and I followed him in this. Indeed with a career in the avantgarde to think about it was expedient to consider things in an isolated, fragmentary way, otherwise one's ideas would tend to coincide with other people's ideas which would lead to the charge of banality and of being an 'epigone'. So in setting the first paragraph I followed Pound's instruction 'to keep on re-reading the whole digest until he understands', and thus hit on a rendering which reflects Pound's 'mantric' interpretation of the text although this interpretation was unknown to me at the time.

An attempt to reform the first two paragraphs of The Great Learning

'If a textbook is too summary, pupils will be able to twist its meaning; if a law is too concise, the people dispute its intentions' – (Han Fei). Shelves full of Chinese scholars' tracts and a fair number of European translations prove the applicability of this legalist thesis to *The Great Learning*. A literal translation of the first two paragraphs yields:
'*The Great Learning*'s way consists in : polishing bright virtue; caring for the people; resting in the highest good.

'Knowing where to rest one has certainty. Being certain one can be calm. Being calm one can have peace. Having peace one can lay plans. Laying plans one can succeed.'

In class society there is no literature or philosophy above classes, and we have seen Confucius's class standpoint above –

he stood on the side of the slave-owning class, which was basically finished but still fighting for survival. From the politics of the present-day ruling class – the bourgeoisie, which is also basically finished but still fighting for survival – we know that 'caring for the people' means dividing them and playing them off against each other so that they don't rise against their oppressors. The imperialists stockpile armaments and murder millions in the name of 'peace' – all they want is to continue their exploitation of working people and underdeveloped countries in 'peace'. The only 'plans' the bourgeoisie make are plans for the further exploitation and oppression of working people, and as for 'success', in bourgeois society your success is measured by your parasitism and profitability.

Let's see how pupil Pound twists the meaning to suit his own ends:

'*The Great Learning* takes root in clarifying the way wherein the intelligence increases through the process of looking straight into one's own heart and acting on the result; it is rooted in watching with affection the way people grow; it is rooted in coming to rest, being at ease in perfect equity.

'Know the point of rest and then have an orderly mode of procedure; having this orderly procedure one can "grasp the azure", that is, take hold of a clear concept; holding a clear concept one can be at peace internally; being thus calm one can keep one's head in moments of danger; he who can keep his head in the presence of a tiger is qualified to come to his deed in due hour.'

Pound's version is tailored to fit his idea of a 'conspiracy of intelligence' to protect Order and Civilisation against the onslaught of the 'mob'. He makes intelligence a matter of introspection. He advocates detachment: an inner sanctum of 'perfect equity' where he reclines at ease 'watching with affection' (as if through a window) the struggles of the people. His 'calm' is the calmness of intellectual superiority; his 'peace' is internal. Only along this road can one 'qualify' to take action.

In 1972 I and the Scratch Orchestra were offered the oportunity to present these two paragraphs in a Promenade Concert at the Albert Hall, London. For this occasion I came up with yet another 'translation' of *The Great Learning*. By this time our political consciousness had been at least awakened and we were taking the first steps along the road of developing political discussion and music-making in the service of the proletarian revolution. Taking as our guideline Chairman Mao's thesis 'Works of art that do not serve the struggle of the broad masses can be transformed into works of art that do', we devised a performance which was formally much more disciplined than the original and which included banners bearing four slogans which expressed our feelings about revolution and the *Great Learning*. These banners were banned from the performance by the BBC, who also censored the programme note to remove all political statements except such as were smuggled into the translation. Here is the new 'translation' together with the slogans:

'*The Great Learning* means raising your level of consciousness by getting right to the heart of a matter and acting on your conclusions. *The Great Learning* is rooted in love for the broad masses of the people. The target of *The Great Learning* is justice and equality, the highest good for all.'

First slogan: 'Make the past serve the present.'

Second slogan: 'Revolution is *The Great Learning* of the present.'

Third slogan: 'A revolution is not a dinner party, it is an insurrection, an act of violence by which one class overthrows another.'

Fourth slogan: 'Apply Marxism-Leninism-Mao Tsetung Thought in a living way to the problems of the present.'

'We know our stand (on the side of the working and oppressed people) and so our aim is set (the overthrow of monopoly capitalism). Our aim being set we can appraise the situation. We appraise the situation and so we are relaxed and ready. We are relaxed and ready and so we can plan ahead despite all danger. Planning ahead despite all danger we shall accomplish our aim.'

I now consider that this effort to 'reform' *The Great Learning* needs to be just as severely criticised as does the work in its original form. In order to harmonise the reactionary ideology of *The Great Learning* with the revolutionary ideology of Marxism-Leninism we were obliged to stand on our heads, and from such a contorted position one can perform no useful service to the revolution. Capitalism cannot be reformed, it must be overthrown. Bourgeois ideology cannot be reformed, it must be smashed. The attempt to reform *The Great Learning* was a logical consequence of a fundamentally 'reformist' attitude which reaches far back into my work as an avantgardist in the '60s and permeates the activities of the Scratch Orchestra (for whom most of *The Great Learning* was written), from its inception up until the time when it began to liberate itself from bourgeois ideology.

What were these 'reforms' that we struggled for in the Scratch Orchestra, and that find their expression in the paragraphs of *The Great Learning*? They are reforms in the interest of certain oppressed individuals. We wanted to break the monopoly of a highly-trained elite over the avantgarde, so we made a music in which 'anyone' could participate regardless of their musical education. We wanted to abolish the useless intellectual complexity of the earlier avantgarde, and make music which was quite concretely 'simple' in its assault on the senses. We wanted to devise a kind of music that would release the initiative of the participants.

In breaking out of the elite we succeeded only in forming a kind of commune and were just as isolated as before. In rejecting intellectual complexity we landed ourselves in situations of brutal chaos in which mystical introspection supervened as a method of self-preservation. And in releasing the initiative of the performers we slipped into the cult of individualism. Hippy communes, mysticism, individualism – our various 'reforms' led us straight into a number of cul-de-sacs of bourgeois ideology that are being widely promoted today.

The ideology of Reformism has a class character; a bourgeois class character

People who set out to reform some of the blatant evils of bourgeois society often do so with the 'best of intentions' and think like we did that they are acting at least in the interests of some oppressed individuals in society. (In the case of social workers, etc., many believe that they are working on behalf of the drastically oppressed sections of the working class with which they come in contact.) Actually such people are carrying out the wishes of the ruling class, of the bourgeoisie. They are the more often than not deluded servants of the bourgeoisie. Reformism is an ideological trend emanating from the bourgeoisie. The bourgeoisie would like nothing better than that the evil symptoms of oppression and exploitation would disappear while the facts of oppression and exploitation remain. The very life of the oppressing and exploiting classes depends on their ability to conceal and mystify their true character. This ability is now wearing very thin. The oppressed and exploited classes are learning in great numbers that they cannot place any faith in promises of reform, whether these promises come from Social Democrats, Divine Light Missionaries, Revisionists or Fascists. They are learning that only through building their own organisations, the organisations of the working class, the genuine communist parties, can the reasonable course be put into practice: the course of proletarian socialist revolution. In the context of this learning, the mystical delights of *The Great Learning* are just butterflies in a blast-furnace.

Criticise The Great Learning from the standpoint of the working class

A reformed *Great Learning* can never be more than an armour-plated butterfly, and for this reason I decided to present the work in future in its unreformed state. No longer do I want to conceal the facts about bourgeois society, I want to expose them. My standpoint in criticising *The Great Learning* is the standpoint of the working class. For the working class *The Great Learning* is – or would be if they ever got to hear it – a piece of inflated rubbish which obviously has no role to play in their struggles; its role is to promote and consolidate bourgeois ideas in one guise or another amongst the intelligentsia.

Through my position as a bourgeois composer I have the right (which is denied to the vast majority of musicians employed by capitalist and state-supported enterprises under the dictatorship of the bourgeoisie) to express my ideas about my own work and those of other bourgeois composers in this form. I hope that in doing so I can promote amongst progressive people a conscious and critical attitude – and finally an attitude of rejection – towards bourgeois music and encourage them to turn their attention to, and integrate themselves with, the progressive forces in present-day society, namely the politics and culture of the working class in its upsurge to wrest political power from the hands of the monopoly capitalist class.

27·3·74

Participating in the Berlin performance of The Great Learning *was a painful and – as it seemed – debilitating experience for me. Holding the view that music's main function is to bring people together, to unite them, it was a contradictory situation to have to direct a performance – which had to be a 'good' performance so that people could get to grips with its content – for the sole purpose of leading the audience, through the accompanying article, to repudiate that content. A 'good' performance is one in which the musicians and audience are totally engaged. In contravening this principle – by disengaging the audience – I had set myself the job of launching a sizeable lead balloon. I accomplished this quite successfully and it was a worried little audience that wended their way out of the hall at the end. This disturbed me; I wished I had had something better to offer, something which we could have united around. Then I reflected (on the basis of some quite concrete experience) that if I had had such a work ready it would doubtless not have been performed in those circumstances, and this depressed me still further. Later I realised the cause of these depressions: I was clinging very tenaciously to the role of the bourgeois composer. Shortly after the concert,* Peking Review *brought out a further article on the subject of criticising Confucius, this one by an old professor who had previously espoused the Confucian cause, just as I had. What he wrote inspired me greatly. I realised that the business of changing one's class stand, remoulding one's world outlook, is no easy thing, no 'lover's bed', but a long and complicated process of struggle: no 'benevolence and righteousness' about it. This struggle may be invigorating or painful or both by turns. On the personal level it brings about important changes: it gradually breaks down all complacency, all loneliness in the process of integrating with the working people, joining the fight to* change the world and shatter the present oppressive conditions finally. In this fight there is, besides hardship and sacrifice, great companionship and great happiness.

Professor Feng Yu-lan of Peking University Department of Philosophy is an old man, but not too old to be warmed by a new world and new ideas as these emerge through the difficult struggle against the old world and its rotten ideas. After his lecture denouncing Confucius he said:

'When the mass movement to criticise Lin Piao and Confucius started last autumn, I was at first rather uneasy. I said to myself: now I'm for it. Before the Great Cultural Revolution started I had always revered Confucius. Now, there is going to be criticism of Lin Piao and criticism of Confucius and the worshipping of Confucius, this means I will also be criticised.

'On second thoughts, however, I found this frame of mind wrong . . . I should join with the revolutionary masses in criticising Lin Piao, criticising Confucius and criticising the worship of Confucius.

'When the university leadership knew how I felt, it encouraged me to speak at a meeting of faculty members and students of the philosophy department on my present understanding of Confucius. . . . As I worked on the speech, my misgivings gradually disappeared. . . . In the concluding portion of the speech I said:

' ". . .I'm nearly eighty and have worked for half a century on the history of Chinese philosophy. It makes me very happy to be able to live to see this revolution, and to take part in it makes me feel all the happier." After I delivered my speech at the meeting, the response I got was a great encouragement to me.' (69)

Notes

1. Morley College in south London was founded in 1889 for the education and recreation of working men and women. Its aim, like that of the whole 'workers' education' movement of the last century, was the inculcation of bourgeois values in the working class. This function has now been taken over by the state education system and these days it's rare to find a manual or industrial worker accepting this kind of cultural poor relief from the bourgeoisie.

In 1968, when I was asked to found an Experimental Music Workshop at Morley, there was no question of any working class orientation in my class, or in the college as a whole. The class ran for five years with up to 20 or 30 people involved – musical amateurs, avantgardists from the visual arts, music students (some from the Royal Academy of Music). Many of these went on to join the Scratch Orchestra.

In 1972, partly because of my intended trip to Berlin in 1973, the class was put formally on a collective basis and the level of work and discussion received a great impetus. The principal, Barry Till, closed the class on fatuous grounds (late payment of fees, alleged failure to conform to the advertised syllabus, etc.) in summer 1973. The students opposed this measure strongly, raising the question, 'Whose interests does Morley College serve, the interests of the students or the interests of the bourgeoisie?' and exposing the political nature of the closure.

2. The main purpose of this *Draft Constitution*, apart from a topsy-turvy privilege system whereby the youngest members were given priority in planning concerts (an illusory dictatorship of the least experienced), was to stimulate the orchestra's repertoire. Several categories were proposed : Improvisation Rites (rules to limit musical 'free expression') Scratch Music (little compositions by individuals for themselves to play, simultaneously with others doing likewise, without coordination), Popular Classics (a fragment of a well-known piece would be torn to shreds), Research Projects (see note 12 below), and compositions (by name composers as well as our own). The Orchestra's programmes were selected and com-

posed by choice or random means from the mass of material engendered by these proposals.

3. I don't think this 'achievement' (independence from feudal patronage) can be credited to the composers; rather to the rising bourgeoisie and the music publishers. Beethoven and others benefited to a certain extent from the new relations of production and gave artistic expression to the new ideology.

4. This was true of the avantgarde composers in the orchestra; there was no 'market' for our work, so we got together and did it for our own satisfaction. In England after the war a market for avantgarde music had simply not been developed, as opposed to Germany, where the market had been developed quite energetically through such institutions as the Darmstadt Summer School for New Music and the radio stations. However, an English avantgarde market was slowly developing about the time the Scratch Orchestra was founded (characters like Cage and Stockhausen who had hitherto been ridiculed by the musical press were thenceforth quite seriously promoted), and composers such as Peter Maxwell Davies and Harrison Birtwistle were beginning to compete relatively successfully on this market, at least to the extent of earning a livelihood from their music.

5. The statistics to back up this statement have not been consistently recorded. Its general truth is borne out by the fact that ever-increasing numbers of musicians are not 'properly employed'; these are the semi-professionals who do a day job and supplement their income with musical gigs in the evening. The devaluation of musical skills by mechanical reproduction methods can be seen in the fact that the easy substitution of recorded music for live makes it difficult for club, hotel and restaurant musicians (one of the most oppressed sections of the profession) to take strike action for better pay.

6. This use of the term 'petty-bourgeois' refers to these people's world outlook and cultural aspirations, not to their actual relations of employment. As Marx and Engels say in the *Communist Manifesto* : 'The bourgeoisie has stripped of its halo every occupation hitherto honoured and looked up to with reverent awe. It has converted the physician, the lawyer, the priest, the poet, the man of science, into its paid wage-labourers.' The same is of course true of the students of these professions.

7. This paragraph has been inserted by Eley to replace a lively

digression on the decaying British education system. The excised passage follows :

'But how has the ruling class in general begun to decay and discharge redundant sections into the proletariat? Apart from the general principle explained by Marx one can point to the specific contradiction between the educational system and the changed economic and social conditions. Fundamentally the British system is a product of the nineteenth century when the British national bourgeoisie controlled one quarter of the world's land surface by direct political rule. That is to say, the public schools, the old grammar schools and the universities were designed to provide an elite, mainly for the purposes of administrating this huge empire. The national bourgeoisie learnt the wrong lessons from their Industrial Revolution with regard to educational policy. Since most of the inventions which helped bring about the revolution were made by amateurs, eccentric geniuses, ordinary working men actually in industry, and pure scientists who put their theoretical work first in importance, little thought was given to technological education. Even by the end of the century the result of this neglect for practical education, or vocational education, could be seen in the rapid advance of Germany and USA in the technological field. But there has been consistent sluggishness to keep up ever since. Today the British Empire does not exist, but the educational system still pumps out increasing masses of people with a "liberal" education, with a theoretical bias in science, with few commerical skills. The absorption of such people into industry and administration has however perpetuated the system, despite intermittent revelations of the incompetence of leadership in industry and government. Now that the decay of British national capitalism becomes clear this can no longer continue.

'The whole job-structure of the British bourgeois class of "merit ocrats" – those who have risen through educational qualifications – is being revealed as a house of cards. Today's civil service was distended by personnel expansion in the 1950s and '6os; significantly during the period when the administrative responsibilities of empire were actually diminishing. Now the Tory government is pledged to cut it back. This amounts to official recognition that many bureaucrats hold little more than sinecures. The cut-back in the managerial classes recently has been drastic with many bankruptcies, mergers and much "rationalisation" of industry to increase efficiency. TV documentaries bewail the unhappy lot of managers and executives on the dole (actually cushioned by socialist earnings-related benefits which often enable them to pay their mortgages and maintain quite a high standard of living!). The bolt-hole of higher education for alienated bourgeois intellectuals and artists – universities and colleges – is now choked with the 30-year-olds who got their sinecures in the bonanza period of expansion a few years ago. So many students graduating today are faced with unemployment. Those going through the educational mill now – more would-be meritocrats – look with increasingly jaundiced eye on the still-promised "bright prospects and security" of the glossy brochures. Some science departments now fail to fill their quota of places through lack of applications. Many students opt for the social science field in search, usually unconsciously, for the root ills of British and western social malaise and stagnation. Thus through personal frustration and study many have lost confidence in capitalism (though they add "in its present form", thus showing how misled they are by the propaganda of so-called economists and sociologists, who perpetrate the bogey of Communism and a fictitious "third way out" – "a change of heart in industry" and other idealistic and anarchistic rubbish). But they do experience the objective fact that, as the bourgeoisie itself diminishes through the small fish disappearing down the gullet of worldwide monopolies, there is *no* "room at the top".'

8. In 1970 a group of Yippies, Black Panthers and others (Jerry Rubin, Abbie Hoffmann, Bobby Seale were three of the defendants) were charged with conspiracy, incitement to riot, and contempt of court in the wake of events during the Democratic Convention in Chicago, 1968. Their supporters in England organised this concert at the Round House to raise money for their defence, bail, etc. As far as I remember, the concert made no reference to the issues involved, and our contribution could be described as ostentatiously 'apolitical'.

9. See note 6 and note 32 below.

10. A few members had experienced this even more forcefully a few weeks earlier. On 1 May, Tilbury and Rowe had gathered a small group of members to participate in the Mayday procession of the workers in Southampton. When it came to it they put away their drums and whistles as mere pathetic encumbrances and participated in the demonstration more honourably as ordinary people supporting the workers' cause.

11. Organisationally, these groups were independent of the Scratch Orchestra. P.T.O. (Promenade Theatre Orchestra) consisted of four trained musicians (John White, Chris Hobbs, Alec Hill and Hugh Shrapnel). This disciplined and homogeneous group met

regularly on Sunday afternoons, and also accepted professional engagements. All four wrote compositions for the group – some were long and used systematic processes (e.g. modelled on bell-ringing), others were short, sharp, humorous items, occasionally using popular material.

Harmony Band was an improvisation of 4–6 people gathered around Dave and Diane Jackman. Not trained musicians, their music was fragile, sensitive and exploratory.

Private Company was founded by Michael Chant. The participants contributed their Concrete poetry, spontaneous painting, philosophical speculation and private imagery to create mixed-media performances with a ritualistic atmosphere (candlelight, drinks, special cakes, etc.).

Another sub-group was the pop group CUM.

The climax of sub-group activity in the Scratch Orchestra was the *Wandelkonzert* (promenade concert) at the German Institute on 13 May 1971, in which fourteen groups or individuals (not all were active in the Scratch Orchestra) distributed their activities through seven rooms of the Institute in accordance with a complex overall programme and plan.

12. This concert was one of the Scratch Orchestra's 'Journey Concerts'. These 'Journeys' were products of the Research Project outlined in the *Draft Constitution*. The 'Journey' at the Queen Elizabeth Hall on 23 November was a *Pilgrimage from Scattered Points on the Surface of the Body to the Brain, the Inner Ear, the Heart and the Stomach.* Each member had to plan his own journey and find ways of documenting it musically. The resulting free-for-all was loosely coordinated in the framework provided by specially composed pieces at the beginning and end of the concert: Michael Parson's *Mindfulness Occupied with the Body* and Richard Ascough's *Rationalisation of Realisation.* For good measure four 'popular classics' were thrown in to represent the four inner organs listed in the title: Mahlers *Sixth Symphony*, Terry Riley's *In C*, the song *Boom Bang-a-bang* and Tchaikovsky's *1812 Overture*. If the Research Project of the *Draft Constitution* was flippant, in its practical realisation it turned into a violent, atavistic rejection of any form of scientific investigation. We used scientific terminology to sanctify and embellish our wanton musical 'good time', and in doing so blindly reflected the bankruptcy and academicism of scientific research in bourgeois society, the lion's share of which is devoted to military technology and advanced methods of exploitation and oppression.

13. During the Newcastle tour we were accompanied by a TV crew under the direction of a student from the Munich film school. This student, Hanne Boenisch, took a serious attitude to the Orchestra's activities and interviewed a large number of members, insisting on discovering the idea behind their participation in the Orchestra. She wanted to know what social significance we thought our work had, and how we saw it developing in the future. Some members cooperated only half-heartedly, but the more conscious members grappled with her questions. Her presence, and the presence of her crew, were an important additional factor in breaking down the discussion taboo.

14. The passage referred to is near the end of the Introduction in Mao Tsetung's *Talks at the Yenan Forum on Literature and Art* :
'I came to feel that compared with the workers and peasants the unremoulded intellectuals were not clean and that, in the last analysis, the workers and peasants were the cleanest people and, even though their hands were soiled and their feet smeared with cowdung, they were really cleaner than the bourgeois and petty-bourgeois intellectuals. That is what is meant by a change in feelings, a change from one class to another. If our writers and artists who come from the intelligentsia want their works to be well received by the masses, they must change and remould their thinking and their feelings. Without such a change, without such remoulding, they can do nothing well and will be misfits.'

15. The opera *Sweet F.A.* (taking its title from the Greg Bright piece that triggered the trouble in Newcastle) was composed collectively after the Discontent meetings. The five scenes represented the five concerts we did in the Newcastle area. The idea and its speedy realisation were stimulated by a large prize offered by an Italian organisation for such a work. *Sweet F.A.* didn't get the prize, and only two scenes from the opera were ever performed. These were : the scene mentioned by Eley, which we staged in two completely different musical versions, and the final scene, which was largely the work of Chris May and included a series of 12 large paintings by the artists in the orchestra. These pieces formed an important part of our repertoire in the following months, dealing as they did with the class struggle as we ourselves had experienced it, and designed as they were to stimulate the musical proficiency of the group.

16. In May 1942 the Chinese Communist Party organised a three-week forum on literature and art. Chairman Mao gave the opening and closing speeches, pointing out the general line that the forum

should take and summing up the results. The forum took place in Yenan, a town in China's northwest. Yenan was the centre of operations for the Communist leadership in the Anti-Japanese war of 1937–45 and the capital of the Shensi-Kansu-Ninghsia Border Region, one of the liberated areas under the provisional government of the Communists. It should cause no surprise that the Chinese Communist Party could find the time in the thick of war to run a three-week forum on literature and art. Culture is as vital to human survival as food and drink; man's so-called spiritual needs are just as real as his material ones, and there is no sharp dividing line between the two. Mao put this point across very incisively when he wrote (in 1944), 'An army without culture is a dull-witted army, and a dull-witted army cannot defeat the enemy.'

17. It was in 1967, during the Great Proletarian Cultural Revolution in China, that *China Pictorial* reprinted the *Talks* as a special supplement to celebrate their 25th anniversary. The *Talks* were an effective weapon in the Cultural Revolution not because of any magical properties but because of their firm proletarian line and their sharp dialectical materialist analysis. These qualities are vital in the struggle of the working class to exercise leadership in all fields and prevent the bourgeoisie from staging a comeback by usurping positions of authority in fields of culture and ideology. By the time the 30th anniversary of the *Talks* came round (1972), artists the world over were tackling the problems of applying the *Talks* to the concrete conditions of their own countries and their own work. To name two examples : in West Berlin a conference was called by the Communist student organisation KSV to study and apply the *Talks*; in London the Scratch Orchestra Ideological Group were studying the *Talks* collectively over a relatively long period. One thing that the Cultural Revolution had brought home to us very forcefully was the need to develop criticism of bourgeois culture : we too need to attack the 'ghosts and monsters' in our cultural environment. We should tie the label GHOST to the tails of those artistic and intellectual trends that promote the ideology of anarchism and reformism, and brand the word MONSTER on the faces of those artistic and intellectual trends that promote the ideology of fascism.

18. This was hearsay from a source I had and have no reason to doubt. Cage denies that such boycotting took place, maintaining that the incident in question occurred in connection with a Stockhausen concert.

19. Kurt Schwertsik is an Austrian composer and hornist who saw clearly the growing alienation of the avantgarde from working musicians and the music-loving audience. In the sixties he became interested in light music and dropped out of the avantgarde, earning his livelihood as an orchestral hornplayer in Vienna.

20. The high standard and unique qualities of this American pianist's playing and personality had a large influence on the piano compositions of Cage and Stockhausen and a number of other composers. He has been a close collaborator of Cage's since around 1950. In recent years he has virtually abandoned piano playing to devote himself to live electronic performance.

21. Tilbury quotes Deryck Cooke's remarks appreciatively because they 'swim against the tide' of current bourgeois musicological theory. Cooke's lament is justified, but when it comes to a statement of his own musicological theories, there is little there that a materialist could support. His definition of music as 'the expression of man's deepest self' betrays an idealist world outlook which sees the highest reality deep in 'man's' soul and not in the outside world. For a materialist, intellectual and artistic activity is a partial and partisan reflection or expression of objective reality, in particular the objective realities of social life. These realities, at least since the emergence of class societies on page one of recorded history, make it quite impossible to speak of 'man' in the abstract, above class. Cooke's use of this term is an example of the partisan character of his own intellectual activity : it is in the interests of the bourgeois class that he glosses over the question of class.

22. Cage's intention seems to be to reflect mechanically, 'unconsciously' (that is with no purposeful compositional intervention) the present stage of the historical development of the musical material, and thus cover up the decisive factor in the historical development of the musical material, namely social development and conscious participation. In this he mirrors the 'objectivity' of those bourgeois scientists who mechanically assemble and process tons of data : their 'objectivity' is a veil to conceal the class standpoint from which their researches are carried out.

23. Cage's mumbo-jumbo about self-centred sounds should stimulate us to clarify the actual mode of existence of sounds. Our concept of sound derives from our faculty of hearing, which in turn probably evolved as a mechanism for detecting and evaluating a particular range of matter-in-motion phenomena. Sound is audible

vibrations in a medium, produced by some form of activity. We have developed activities specifically to produce sounds which convey through their character and combination our experience of the world as we know it from our particular standpoint. These activities constitute music-making, a specifically human affair, to which we may obviously compare a whole range of non-human and non-audible activities (bird 'song', 'music of the spheres', the 'music of your smile', etc.) but which is firmly rooted in and cannot be detached from the social life of human beings. Cage calling his music 'sounds' (rather than music) therefore represents an attempt to remove it from the human sphere (categorically impossible, since the activities of human beings can never be non-human), from which he promises himself a double advantage : (a) it would absolve him from his human responsibility for his actions as a human being, and (b) it would give his music the superhuman 'objective' authority of a phenomenon of (blind, unconscious) nature. In fact, man and his thinking are themselves a part of 'nature', whose products are by no means all wise, harmonious and graceful, as can be seen from such blatant examples as the dinosaur and Cage's metaphysics.

24. Engels expressed the dialectical relationship between freedom and necessity as follows : 'Freedom is the appreciation of necessity'. For instance : freedom for the working class can only consist in recognising the historical necessity of overthrowing capitalism and actually doing so.

25. Actually the capitalists' first commandment is 'maximise profits' which means essentially 'maximum exploitation of labour'. The so-called 'law of supply and demand' is a complex affair of creating, conquering, dividing up and destroying markets, involving cutthroat rivalry amongst the bourgeoisie and a nearly total disregard of the 'demand', the actual needs of the human consumers who make up these markets. The capitalist (say, the grainhoarder in India, will not supply goods where there is a demand for them (grain to the starving) unless the rate of profit is adequate (to his greed).

26. Cage generally disclaims any subjective intention in his work ('just let the sounds be sounds', and so on). At his boldest he might say that he wanted his music to make people free. Its effect is the opposite : entangling people.

27. The Nazi campaign against 'degenerate' art is viewed differently by different classes. For the bourgeoisie, the main victims in this campaign were the bourgeois avantgardists : Klee, Kandinsky, Schönberg and others whose work did in fact reflect the ideological

degeneration of the bourgeoisie into metaphysics. From the proletarian point of view, the main victims were the Communist artists of the Weimar Republic : Georg Grosz, Käthe Kollwitz, Hanns Eisler, Bertold Brecht. The German capitalists brought the fascists to power as a last resort, a desperate gamble to stave off collapse. On the cultural front their attack was two-pronged : on the one hand they suppressed the culture (the bourgeois avantgarde) that reflected the bankruptcy and weakness of their own class, and on the other they suppressed the culture that reflected the growing consciousness and militancy of their enemy, the working class. The anti-semitic line of the campaign was just a red herring. There was no need for the Nazis to ban Mahler's works, for instance, but they did because he was a Jew. Possibly the main advantage the Nazis derived from their racist anti-semitic line on the ideological front was that it enabled them to outlaw Marxism (Communism) not because it was proletarian, but because Marx was a Jew!

When the Darmstadt Summer School for New Music was founded after the war its claimed intention was to reinstate and develop that music which had suffered persecution at the hands of the Nazis. Because the West German state was again a bourgeois state, the Darmstadt Summer School of course reinstated the *bourgeois* composers who had been victimised by the Nazis, not the socialist composers. Darmstadt propagated the so-called Second Viennese School – Schönberg, Berg and Webern – and offered encouragement to young composers – Boulez, Stockhausen and Nono became the leading names – to proceed further along the road of serial music. What they turned out was a kind of atomised 'music for its own sake', appreciated only by a tiny circle of composers, musicologists and their admirers, plus a certain number of even younger musicians who, because they felt alienated by the sterility and banality of the musical establishment, were attracted by certain progressive catchwords current in Darmstadt circles. These catchwords were, as far as I remember, 'science', 'democracy', 'consciousness', 'progress', and we were to see them all turn into their opposites in subsequent years : mysticism, dictatorship, anti-consciousness and reaction. In the climate of political reaction of the 1950's, with the Cold War, the death of Stalin and the growth of a new bourgeoisie in the Soviet Union, the Darmstadt school flourished. By 1970, when the world political climate had changed dramatically for the better, with national liberation struggles on the increase throughout the world, great successes of the Great Proletarian Cultural Revolution in China and growing working class militancy in the imperialist heartlands, Darmstadt had become a stagnant backwater.

114

28. Karl Marx, *Contribution to the Critique of Political Economy*, Preface.

29. Karl Marx, *Capital*, Vol. I.

30. In a sense this music is indeed 'derivative', but it was wrong to use this word, which has a pejorative character in bourgeois criticism. In fact there is no art production that is not derived in some way from things that went before, and above all there is no art that is not 'derived' from social practice. It was wrong to 'knock' popular music in a general way because the vast mass of working musicians, employed in popular music under very oppressive conditions, represent the basic musical resources of the working class. Despite the restrictive relations of production, which hamper cultural development just as they hamper economic development, this mass of working musicians has achievements to its credit, especially technical achievements. Genuine artistic achievements on a grand scale are of course not possible under the dictatorship of a degenerate bourgeois ideology.

31. John Cage, *Defence of Satie*. (A lecture delivered at Black Mountain College in 1948.)

32. I was not clear on the class character of this audience when I wrote the talk. The audience for classical music consists largely of educated and professional workers – wage-slaves all, despite their non-participation in manual labour. When people speak of the 'bourgeois audience' this refers to the fact that this audience is to a great extent under the influence of bourgeois ideas and claims the cultural privileges that are held out to them to distinguish them and divide them from the manual workers. The 'snobbish' character of a certain part of the audience derives from its acceptance of these and other privileges in return for non-participation in the class struggle on the side of the workers. However, at the present time large numbers – including some of those that enjoy bourgeois music – of these non-manual workers (civil servants, teachers, etc.) are becoming class conscious and are adopting the methods of class struggle that were previously thought to be peculiar to the industrial proletariat and other manual workers. For instance, they go on strike. In proportion as this becomes the general trend the fascination of bourgeois concerts – all that wholesomeness, delight, inspiration, etc. – is likely to grow continually paler.

33. Since writing this talk such fantasies have lost all their charm for me. More often than not they are not only distorting the truth, they are deliberately spreading metaphysical or even fascist ideas.

34. 1848–49 is often referred to as the 'Year of Revolutions'. 1848 saw the first ever armed rising of the proletariat as a class acting on its own behalf, in Paris June 23–26. This rising was brutally suppressed by the bourgeoisie.

In 1849 there were risings of a different type : popular, uncoordinated risings in several German states in support of the new (bourgeois) Constitution adopted by the parliament in Frankfurt in March 1849, which various monarchs had refused to recognise. The rising in Dresden was put down by Prussian troops on 9 May 1849.

Wagner was director of the Dresden Opera at the time and was filled with enthusiasm for the revolution, which he hoped would open the way to the realisation of his artistic dreams. He participated in the rising and as a result spent the next 13 years in exile bitterly regretting it all and servilely begging forgiveness. His political views were a hotch-potch and his fidelity to them completely unstable. (The ideological and political content of his music is another subject, and can't be dealt with here.)

Much stauncher in his support of the bourgeois revolution was Wagner's assistant in Dresden, Röckel. He spent 13 years in prison for his part in the rising and resolutely refused to sue for pardon or renege on his views.

35. Marx was persistently hounded by the authorities in 1848 and 1849. Banished from Belgium early in 1848, he made his way to Cologne via Paris. In Cologne he edited the *Neue Rheinische Zeitung* for almost a year. During this time he was put on trial, but was acquitted in February 1849. In May he was banished from Germany and went to Paris, was banished from Paris and went to London, where he lived for the rest of his life. (For a short account of Marx's life, see Lenin's essay *Karl Marx*.) The reason he was thus hounded was that the theses set out in the *Communist Manifesto*, drawn up by Marx and Engels early in 1848, were consistently borne out by the historic events of that year, and Marx was contributing continuously to the growing consciousness of the rising workers.

36. This is one-sided. Primarily, capitalists regard the people as labour power capable of producing 'surplus value', from which they derive profit. Part of this surplus value goes to expand production, and expanding production sends the capitalists in search of markets

to consume their multiplying products, and where no legitimate market exists they use advertising techniques and other means to create an artificial one. Cigarettes are a better example than plastic bottles and white bread, because while bringing in vast profits, cigarettes not only don't benefit the people, they actually harm them.

37. This sentence is incorrect. In fact there can only be socialist construction when the capitalist system is overthrown.

An economic system such as capitalism or socialism protects itself with a political dictatorship, in which one or more classes (within which there may well be democratic institutions) holds sway over the rest (for whom these democratic institutions are little more than scraps of paper).

The capitalist system is protected by the political dictatorship of the monopoly capitalist class, exercised through its organ the bourgeois state, with its 'democratically elected' government and its obviously anti-democratic armed forces and police. By no stretch of the imagination can your right to vote once every five years or so be considered a meaningful participation in the political affairs of a country, whereas the 'right' of the police to arrest and intern people for doing nothing whatever ('creating an obstruction', etc.) is well known to all. These are features of the dictatorship of the bourgeoisie. Its aim is to hamper the development of socialism.

A socialist economy must equally be protected by a dictatorship, whose aim is to prevent the re-emergence of capitalism. This dictatorship is the dictatorship of the proletariat, which deprives the bourgeoisie and other exploiting classes of all political rights. Only under such a dictatorship can socialism be built. This goes for both economic affairs and cultural affairs. Hence the need for any socialist composer worth his salt to do propaganda for socialist revolution and the dictatorship of the proletariat.

38. When the capitalist class holds political power it takes all available measures to censor and stifle proletarian revolutionary art. This is its first law in the field of art and it is a political law. The same applies in a socialist country like China. True, after liberation the business of rescuing the economy from the ravages of war took precedence over cultural matters, and despite a healthy growth of proletarian culture the art of the exploiting classes continued to dominate the stage. The Great Proletarian Cultural Revolution set the course for rectifying this contradictory state of affairs, and now if works by Chinese artists show traces of bourgeois ideas or smack of capitalist restoration they are criticised and if necessary

suppressed. If such works are allowed to see the light of day, then only for the sake of denouncing them and preventing the further growth of such trends. The reasons for this are political : if bourgeois art were allowed to flourish it would undermine the dictatorship of the proletariat.

39. 'Necessity for Change' is the title of a document prepared by the Internationalists for the 'Necessity for Change' Conference, held in London in August 1967. In this Marxist–Leninist document the aspiration of the youth and student movement of the '60s to actively participate in and change things is summed up. Its first sentence is : 'Understanding requires an act of conscious participation, an act of finding out.' The first part of the document deals with the phenomenon of 'anti-consciousness' referred to in the talk.

40. Utopia, literally, 'nowhere'; a never-never land purified of all social injustice. In the Communist Manifesto of 1848 Marx and Engels roundly criticised the 'Utopian Socialism' of such bourgeois thinkers as Owen and Fourier, whose tendency was to 'invent' ideal social systems without taking into account the actual laws governing the development of society. By these means they lulled the workers with sweet dreams instead of arming them with correct theory to guide them in their battles in the real world. To 'utopian socialism' Marx and Engels opposed 'scientific socialism', and made it their business to investigate the laws of social development and place their discoveries in the service of the working class and indicate the immediate line of advance. (See Engels, *Socialism: Utopian and Scientific*.)

41. The formulations in the following three paragraphs are taken directly from a letter from Wolff received in response to a request for programme notes for the piece.

42. Most of this work had actually been done when I proposed the work for inclusion in a Scratch Orchestra concert in Birmingham in December 1972. On that occasion, despite my impassioned resistance, the Scratch Orchestra finally barred the work from the concert on the general grounds that it ridiculed the Chinese revolution (making it out to be a question of cows and condoms) and did not mention the role of the Communist Party and the fighting spirit of the masses. Whether or not Wolff had the intention of ridiculing the revolution is a secondary matter, the main thing being the effect that the piece has. Everyone knows that the most ridiculous statements

are usually made with a serious mien; in fact this seriousness is no small ingredient in the ridiculousness of the effect. The fluency of Wolff's statements reported in the programme note must be regarded with suspicion. Either it conceals a real naivety (which needs to be overcome, as there is no room for naivety in the struggle against bourgeois ideology) or he is pretending to be naive in order to ridicule the Chinese revolution.

43. Rzewski here offloads his responsibility for the contradiction (he calls it 'ambiguity') between the subjective character of the piece and the political events to which it draws attention on to the shoulders of the interpreter.

Further material from Rzewski on *Coming Together* ('from a letter accompanying the score') was published in the third issue of the magazine *Soundings*. The technical procedures employed in the piece are described in more detail, and in the final paragraph more light is shed on Rzewski's attitude. Here is the extract :

'The text for *Coming Together* is taken from a letter written by Sam Melville from Attica Correctional Facility in the spring of 1971. Sam Melville was murdered by the state in the assault on Attica last autumn.

'The score for *Coming Together* consists of a single melody written in the bass clef. There are several ways of interpreting this piece, depending on the number of persons available. The simplest possible version can be done by one person who both plays the melody as it is written and recites the text at the same time. I have performed it this way at the piano. Ideally, however, there should be one person reciting the text and a number of musicians accompanying him in the following way :

'One musician at least plays the melody straight through in very strict time on a bass instrument, preferably electric bass or bass guitar. The others do not play at all at first but enter gradually, playing long notes in the beginning with silences between them, then gradually shortening the durations of the long notes and the silences so that they become notes of medium duration, groups of notes, short melodies and fragments of melodies and so on. Most of these notes are octave doublings of notes in the bass line which are then sustained for as long as the player wishes before going on to the next doubling. What happens is this, that a number of melodies arises, as many as there are players, the sum of which however is as it were a freely articulated orchestration of the principal melody. In addition, however, the musicians should try to interpolate freely improvised passages that depart from this rule, with the condition that they do not get lost. It is very hard not to get lost, so that to be free in this situation really requires a struggle. As the music approaches the end (the piece lasts about half an hour) the durations become shorter and shorter so that for the last section everyone is playing in unison or octaves. Dynamics are free, although basically loud, and a percussion part may be improvised, as long as it helps to keep people together.

'Regarding your comment (presumably referring to the editor of *Soundings* No. 3) on the pessimism presently affecting American composers, I would only like to point out that, where this phenomenon is manifested, it is usually a trivial and naive pessimism which does not really reflect their long-term attitudes, and it can be corrected by further discussion of the question, "Whom are we serving?" in particular, and by further politicisation in general. A new stage of revolutionary optimism is now beginning among American artists, I think, although this has to be expressed in concrete actions, and although a certain component of intellectual pessimism should perhaps, at the same time, be retained. Pessimism is the basic philosophy of the ruling class, for whom change can only be for the worse, whereas for us the prospects for change are good, although this may require long duration and effort.'

Rzewski's assessment of pessimism as a characteristic of the ruling class in its period of decline is correct, so why does he plead for the retention of 'a certain component of intellectual pessimism'? This shows an ambivalence in Rzewski's attitude.

44. In implying that the provisional IRA is a 'terrorist' organisation I fell victim to bourgeois propaganda. The real terrorists are the British Government and their army in Ulster. There may be disagreement as to their aims and tactics, but the provisional IRA are organising armed struggle against British imperialism, against the forces of reaction, and to this extent they are playing a progressive role.

45. Thank heaven for that! But the fairy story element should have been criticised anyway, for its utopian (see note 40) tendencies. To sing, to a middle class American audience, obsessed as they are by hygiene, about the revolutionary necessity to wash your hands before meals – this crassly divorces the Chinese revolution from the concrete conditions of the West.

46. Goffredo Petrassi, 'grand old man' among Italian composers, opened the symposium with the remark that it was about a 'false

problem', that notation was not in any way a real 'problem' facing composers today.

47. A clear example is Stockhausen's *First Piano Piece*. It sounds like a fairly haphazard juxtaposition of notes and chords, but involves the pianist in very abstruse technical problems, such as playing a ten-note chord where each note must have a different degree of loudness, or passages where changes of tempo are expressed as complicated ratios (e.g. 11 quavers in the time of twelve, within which there may well be other complicated ratios to cope with) in relation to a basic tempo which is 'as fast as possible for the shortest rhythmic values used in the piece'. Another example is Cage's *Music of Changes*. In both these cases the development of notation complexities in line with serial (mathematical) composition technique led to complexities of performance that would not otherwise have arisen and that had no appreciable effect on the sounding result.

48. *Autumn '60 for Orchestra* and *Solo with Accompaniment* are two compositions of mine that fall into this category. Other examples include Pousseur's game-like pieces and much of Christian Wolff's music. In these cases it is not so much that each composition is a unique system, but that the composer develops, over a number of pieces, his own unique system of notation – a kind of hopeful guarantee for the uniqueness of the resulting music, on which the avantgarde composer's reputation depends.

49. 'The Good Old Days' of bourgeois art is what is being referred to here, i.e. the period when artists were voicing the aspirations of the ascendant (progressive in that context) bourgeoisie. An example of such progressive aspirations is the slogan 'liberty, fraternity, equality' under which the French bourgeoisie mobilised the masses to overthrow the reactionary monarchy in the French Revolution. The bourgeoisie are still touting this when they talk of the 'free world' and the 'western democracies'. Working people and other progressive people are pretty clear as to the fraudulence of these claims today. They ask : 'Free for whom? Democratic for whom?' and face the fact that we live and work under the dictatorship of the bourgeoisie. They are now demanding freedom and democracy for the working people, which means smashing up the freedom and democracy of the bourgeoisie.

50. This mechanical notion has cropped up twice in this talk. It omits to mention that our ideas about the world, our world outlook,

are determined by the social position from which we view it, by our class standpoint. There is no abstract knowledge, no abstract right and wrong, only partisan knowledge, class ideas.

51. George Brecht, American artist, was active in the 'Happenings' period of avantgarde art in the early sixties. His work has had an influence on such movements as Concept Art and Minimal Art.

52. While working on *Treatise* I was preoccupied with the philosophical writings of Ludwig Wittgenstein in the fields of logic and language. One of Wittgenstein's sources was the German philosopher Gottlob Frege (1848–1925), particularly his book on the Foundations of Mathematics.

53. This remark does *not* account for the 'tenacity of bourgeois ideas in the avantgarde'. It's not the ideas that are tenacious, it's the avantgardists : they cling to the ideas to maintain their feeling of self-importance. The remark quoted was prompted by the fact that from 1962–70 (with a few longish breaks) I worked in an office as a graphic designer, pursuing music as a spare-time activity. Hence the escapist character of this music; it was a 'fantasy' to which I attached vast importance. It helped me to overlook the fact that I was just a wage-slave of the capitalists like millions of others.

54. Carpitezza (he must have been a professor of ethnomusicology) had played a tape of a man of the Hukwe tribe (in Africa, I think) singing to the accompaniment of a log drum. The lecture brought in four independent transcriptions of this song by students in an American university, and pointed out the vast differences of interpretation displayed in these. 'Interpretation' here referred not to any understanding of the meaning or function of the song but simply to the physical data on the tape, which the students 'interpreted' in the light of their existing 'eurocentric' framework of formal criteria for evaluating musical sounds.

55. Professor Stefani (Italian musicologist) gave the leading speech on musicology, the longest and most systematic.

56. Robert Ashley is an American avantgarde composer teaching in a Californian university. I don't remember the subject of his speech, and as for his political statements I only retain an impression of his desperation at the bankruptcy of bourgeois culture in the U.S.

57. During the symposium there were concerts in the evenings. At one of these concerts Earle Brown's composition *Synergy* had been badly performed, and Brown took it upon himself publicly to denounce the Italian composer Franco Evangelisti – in so far as he was responsible for the concert – as dishonest and irresponsible in his attitude, and as having wilfully travestied Brown's intentions with regard to the notation.

58. Kurt Stone, American professor, had pleaded for codification and standardisation of all new notation symbols introduced in new music, on a continuous long-term basis with the aid of government grants, computer time, office staff, etc. If one turned a blind eye to the scandalous waste of money and resources involved, his proposal seemed quite reasonable. It hoped to draw composers and players together to co-operate in solving their problems, etc., etc. However, Stone's proposal drew a lot of censure from the individualistic composers of the avantgarde (people like Ashley). They felt threatened in their 'freedom' to develop personal and unique notation ideas, hating the thought that these might become common property. In the intervening period, I have heard no further news of Stone's project.

59. Widmer was a music teacher or educationalist from a South American country. His talk was about the use of new notation systems for school music.

60. Nattiez was a French-Canadian scientist, who could have carried away any prize offered for abstruse terminology.

61. Because it does not take up the issue of classes in society, this paragraph degenerates into woolliness. (The subsequent paragraphs take a turn for the better.) 'Serving the needs of society' in a bourgeois academic context (like Widmer and Stone) means serving the needs of the ruling class in society, and the more co-operative and 'social' their way of doing this the more effectively their work can be used against the oppressed classes. The most that can be said for such people is that they are serious and workmanlike, and these qualities could become useful to the oppressed classes if these people were to change their class stand. The out and out individualists, on the other hand (whether avantgarde composers or scientists like Nattiez) are not so much serious as fanatical and obsessive, building their careers on 'drunken speculation'.

62. Despite my moralistic exhortations to composers to take 'solemn and searching looks' at their work, etc., this passage still betrays the arrogance of the avantgardist. In offering avantgardists a 'seminal role' I appealed to their vanity, and real progress is out of the question when one's sole basis for unity is bourgeois vanity. I now realise that I capitulated at this point to the ideological climate of the symposium, i.e. I lapsed into a tacit assumption that the bourgeois avantgarde is in some sense a 'vanguard', is 'advanced'. It's not; it's backward. That's its dominant aspect. On the question of what role avantgarde composers can play in the class struggle, it would have been more correct to speak not about 'our ideas' and 'our music', but about the ideas and the music of the militant working class and encourage the composers and others to place their work-potential in the service of that class.

63. This promise is not kept in the article, so I will deal with it here.

Paragraph one of *The Great Learning* opens with a chorus of clicking stones. Then comes an extended organ solo characterised by long, changing conglomerations of notes. Then the chorus, divided into two sections, re-enters. One section speaks the text and the other plays long held notes on all kinds of whistle instruments. The text over, one of the whistlers breaks into a birdsong-like interpretation of a string of graphic 'phrases' derived from Chinese calligraphy, while the other whistlers continue holding their notes. The text is then spoken again and another whistler plays the solo, and so on until all the whistlers have played a solo and the text has been repeated a final time, during which the whistlers all drop out. Thereupon only a three-note organ chord remains and on the striking of a small bell the organ is switched off. The air pressure dies out slowly in the pipes, creating strange sliding sounds which gradually fade to nothing. The effect is extremely solemn and ritualistic, provided, that is, that it is not disrupted by justifiably irreverent laughter. The fragile yet raw naturalistic 'nature' sounds of the stones and whistles sets off the succulent religiosity of the organ solo. The result, if successful : a mystic awe at the grandeur of the universe. Against this backcloth the human element, the speaking chorus, humbly voices its submission. The bell at the end is like a benediction on this quiet submissiveness, and the divine presence fades away about its business. There is no hint of struggle or excitement, and the human element in the piece is of a tameness that would have warmed old Confucius's reactionary heart.

Paragraph two is scored for a number of groups of singers, each accompanied by a drummer and an instrumentalist. The groups (usually four or five groups) are positioned around the hall so as more or less to enclose the audience. The drummers all start together, choosing one out of twenty-six available rhythms. Each drummer acts independently of the others : choosing his own tempo, he repeats his chosen rhythm over and over while the choral group behind him sings through a phrase of long notes, led by the instrumentalist. At the end of each phrase the drummer chooses a new rhythm until he has used up twenty-five of the rhythms. The first drummer to arrive at the last rhythm establishes a tempo to which the other drummers conform as they too arrive at their last rhythms. The drummers thus end the piece with a semblance of unity : they are playing different rhythms but in the same tempo. Throughout the piece the drums dominate; the rising and falling phrases of the voices only just manage to penetrate. Only very occasionally does a chance constellation produce a strong harmonious sonority.

Superficially this stormy piece is the antithesis of the first paragraph, but the essential schema is the same : nature, the stormy racket of the competing drums, again holds sway over the human element, the voices, this time subjugating them by sheer brute violence. Here indeed there is struggle and excitement, the vocal part is taxing in the extreme; but the outcome of the struggle is defeat.

64. See *Peking Review* Nos. 8 and 9, 1974, 'Struggle between Two Lines in the Ideological Sphere during the Spring and Autumn Period and the Warring States Period', by Yang Jung-kuo.

65. The following extract on the May 4th Movement is taken from *Peking Review* No. 19, 1974, page 5. 'In early 1919, not long after the end of World War I, an imperialist conference was convened in Paris to share the spoils – the colonies. This was the so-called Paris Peace Conference. The imperialist countries at the conference arrogantly turned down China's just demands for abrogation of imperialist special rights in Shantung Province. When this news reached China, it aroused the great indignation of the Chinese people. On May 4th that year, patriotic students in Peking held mass meetings and demonstrations in front of Tien An Men. They demanded : "Uphold our sovereignty! Punish the traitors!" and "Down with imperialism and the traitorous government!"

'The movement spread swiftly throughout China and, from June 3rd onwards, workers in Shanghai and other places went on strike and held demonstrations. The working class stood like a giant in the forefront of the struggle against imperialism and feudalism, playing a most powerful part. Stirred by the workers' and students' actions, shopkeepers in all major cities put up their shutters and joined in the struggle. The May 4th Movement thus became a nation-wide revolutionary movement with the proletariat, the petty bourgeoisie and bourgeoisie taking part.

'On the eve of the 55th anniversary of the May 4th Movement this year, the Peking University Committee of the Chinese Communist Youth League and the Students' Union jointly held a commemoration meeting and organised a lecture.

'Basing themselves on what is happening in the current struggle, the students conscientiously studied Chairman Mao's brilliant works *The May 4th Movement* and *The Orientation of the Youth Movement* and reviewed the historical experience of the May 4th Movement. The students came to a profound understanding that the May 4th Movement came into being at the call of the October Revolution and of Lenin. It was at once an anti-imperialist, anti-feudal political movement and a great cultural revolution. With its spearhead directed at the doctrines of Confucius and Mencius, the movement raised the clarion call "Down with the Confucian shop", lit the torch of struggle against Confucius and won magnificent achievements.'

See also Lu Hsun's contribution to the criticism of Confucius, *Confucius in Modern China*, reprinted in *Chinese Literature* No. 4, 1974. The article was written in 1935.

66. *Peking Review* No. 8, 1974, page 8.

67. Anthologised in *Ezra Pound: Selected Prose 1909–1965*, Cookson (ed), Faber 1973.

68. *Literature and Ideology* No. 8, 1971, *The political theme of Ezra Pound's Cantos*.

69. *Peking Review* No. 12, 1974, page 14.

ISBN 978-1-7320986-9-5

Primary Information
155 Freeman Street, Ground Floor
Brooklyn, NY 11222
www.primaryinformation.org

Managing editor (2020): James Hoff
Managing designer (2020): Scott Ponik

Primary Information would like to thank Horace Cardew,
Andrew Fenchel, Luke Fowler, and Rick Myers.

Primary Information is a 501(c)(3) nonprofit organization that receives
generous support through grants from the Michael Asher Foundation,
the Graham Foundation for Advanced Studies in the Fine Arts, the
Greenwich Collection Ltd, the National Endowment for the Arts,
the New York City Department of Cultural Affairs in partnership
with the City Council, the New York State Council on the Arts with
the support of Governor Andrew Cuomo and the New York State
Legislature, the Orbit Fund, the Stichting Egress Foundation, VIA Art
Fund, The Jacques Louis Vidal Charitable Fund, The Andy Warhol
Foundation for the Visual Arts, the Wilhelm Family Foundation, and
individuals worldwide.

Printed in the USA at McNaughton & Gunn